Before Love Can Heal:
When Loving Feels One-Sided

Before Love Can Heal:

When Loving Feels One-Sided

Dr Chuck Carrington

This is a nonfiction work. However, certain sections have been lightly fictionalized or dramatized for illustrative purposes. Any resemblance to actual persons, living or deceased, is purely coincidental.
Copyright © 2025 CP Carrington
all rights reserved
ISBN 979-8-9988624-1-0 (paperback edition)
Printed by Connect Books in the United States of America

Connect Books
USA
PO BOX 903 Wakefield VA. USA 23888
Connectbooks.pub

All rights reserved. No part of this book may be reproduced in any form or by an electronic or mechanical means, including information storage and retrieval systems, without permission in writing from the publisher, except by a reviewer who may quote brief passages in a review.

New International Version® (NIV)

Scripture quotations marked (NIV) are taken from the *Holy Bible, New International Version®, NIV®*. Copyright ©1973, 1978, 1984, 2011 by Biblica, Inc.™ Used by permission. All rights reserved worldwide.

English Standard Version (ESV)

Scripture quotations marked (ESV) are from *The Holy Bible, English Standard Version®*, copyright © 2001 by Crossway, a publishing ministry of Good News Publishers. Used by permission. All rights reserved.

New King James Version® (NKJV)

Scripture quotations marked (NKJV) are from the *New King James Version®*. Copyright ©1982 by Thomas Nelson. Used by permission. All rights reserved.

Unless otherwise indicated, all Scripture quotations are taken from the King James Version (KJV), which is in the public domain. Scripture quotations marked (NIV), (ESV), or (NKJV) are used by permission and are noted accordingly. Some Scripture content may be paraphrased or adapted for clarity and teaching purposes and is not intended to represent a formal translation.

To my best friend, James. I thought of you often while writing this book. I still remember the day you told me you needed a heart change—that somewhere between childhood and adulthood, you had lost what God originally gave you: a heart for others. You said God made your mission clear from that day forward—simple, but profound: *love them well, as Jesus would.* Over the years, I've watched that transformation unfold. I've seen your old heart replaced with a new one. And everyone who knows you says the same thing: *James loves me well.* Well done, my friend.

> *"Create in me a clean heart, O God; and renew a right spirit within me."*

(Psalm 51:10 KJV)

The Reason I Wrote This Book 1

When They First Walked In 3

Chapter 1: The Theology of Agape 13

Chapter 2: The Psychology of the Wounded Self 19

Chapter 3: The Culture of Self Before Sacrifice 29

Chapter 4: Asking the Right Question 37

Chapter 5: I Must Challenge My False Beliefs 49

Chapter 6: I Must Own My Side of the Street 57

Chapter 7 I Must Challenge What I Think I Know 65

Chapter 8 Defining My Marriage 71

Chapter 9 Love That Does Not Wait 79

Chapter 10: What It Does Not Mean 87

Chapter 11: Your Heart Repositioned 97

Chapter 12: *I'll know I loved Well* 105

Six Months Later: 111

Appendix: Power Convictions Reflection Journal 115

Appendix: False Belief Worksheet 119

The Reason I Wrote This Book

This book grew out of a need. As a counselor, I speak to countless couples who come to me in hope of saving their marriage. Many times, they arrive long after all hope seems to be lost. In those moments, my silent prayer is for God to instill two things, first, that He provides them with an extra measure of supernatural patience so that they will not give up before we can get the hard work under way. The second and more selfish part is that he helps me to say something that will inspire them to even come back again.

You see, it's hard to have those exact words when a couple is on their last breath of hope, because there is no magic pill that solves a marriage crisis. By the time most couples come to counseling, they are in a pretty bad place, and the hurt, anger, and resentment is already out of proportion to reality. Fortunately, God is a great script writer. All I need to do is listen. And, like Balaam's donkey in the Old Testament, I had to learn to open my mouth and let the Spirit do the talking. And that is where I learned the Power Convictions. This book takes the prequal, which you likely read, and expands it to explain the entire principle behind the power convictions. I hope you will see why it is necessary to pray before entering into a marriage counseling relationship. There are hard truths that even healthy marriages have difficulty with. And as a Christian counselor, I must speak truth, even if it means making people not like me much. So, this book is born out of necessity. I hope it helps you heal.

PART ONE

The Inner Battle

Before love can heal a marriage, it must confront what is broken within the self. This section explores the internal struggles—shame, false beliefs, emotional wounds, and reactive coping—that keep us trapped. By gaining clarity about the stories we carry, we can begin to make space for real, redemptive love.

When They First Walked In

They were ten minutes late to our session, after arriving fifteen minutes early for their appointment. They had spent all that time arguing in the car out in the parking lot before they finally came in. and from their appearance, they were already exhausted. You could read the state of their marriage in their posture—she sat stiff and defensive, arms crossed tightly over her chest; he leaned back, jaw clenched, eyes darting to the window as if looking for an escape. They weren't speaking to each other.

When I welcomed them into my office, they made polite attempts to smile, but it didn't last long. As soon as they sat down, the silence cracked.

"She just doesn't care," he said, not even looking at her. "Everything I say, she twists. I can't do anything right. I'm tired of being the bad guy."

She let out a sharp breath, almost a laugh. "You're tired? You're tired? I've been carrying this marriage for years. All you ever do is criticize me. You say I twist your words? Maybe if you actually listened instead of lecturing me—"

And we were off.

What followed was a rapid-fire list of grievances: who didn't follow through, who failed to support, who shut down, who overreacted. Their words were full of "you always" and "you never." They were both deeply wounded, but neither could say so without turning it into an accusation.

They wanted help—but they wanted help changing each other.

When I finally interrupted the volley of frustration, I asked one question: "When did you stop being friends?"

They paused. Looked at me. Then looked away from each other again.

"I don't know," she whispered. "I guess when he stopped trying."

"No," he shot back. "When you made everything my fault."

They both slumped back into silence. They weren't ready to see what needed to change—because each one was convinced that the problem lived in the other person.

But I had seen this before. Many times. I knew what they didn't know yet: that healing could begin—not when one person fixed the other, but when each one turned inward and took ownership of their side of the street.

They weren't ready for that truth. Not yet. But we had somewhere to go.

Why Love Isn't Working

You don't pick up a book like this unless something feels broken. Maybe it's your marriage. Maybe it's your spouse. Or maybe, deep down, you know it's something in you. You might still live in the same house, wear the same rings, share the same last name—but the intimacy is gone. The connection feels mechanical. You talk, but not really. You function, but you don't flourish. And the more you try to fix it, the more exhausted, confused, and discouraged you feel.

You are not alone. And more importantly, you are not beyond hope. You are not the only one silently wondering if it's too late or if your efforts even matter. You may have prayed, read books, watched videos, or begged God to change your spouse, only to feel like you're running in place. But something brought you here—to these pages—and I believe that "something" may be God's invitation to start the work somewhere deeper. Somewhere quieter. Somewhere within you.

If you've come looking for a quick solution to make your spouse behave or your feelings return, this book will disappoint you. If your primary goal is to reclaim the comfort of the way things used to be, you might not find that here. But if you are ready to look in the mirror and ask God to change you first—even if your spouse never reads a page of this book—then I believe you're about to see something truly redemptive happen. Not necessarily quick. Not necessarily easy. But beautiful, profound, and Spirit-led.

What If the Problem Isn't What You Think It Is?

We live in a culture that trains us to ask, *"How do I get what I want?"* rather than *"How do I become who I need to be?"* This shift is subtle but catastrophic in relationships. From childhood, we're conditioned to seek convenience, validation, and comfort. We're told that love should feel good, relationships should meet our needs, and anything that hurts must be a sign something's wrong. But in marriage, that mindset is a trap.

We are trained to measure love by feelings, fairness, and fulfillment—as if love is something we fall into and out of depending on how happy or hurt we feel. When love becomes primarily about receiving rather than giving, it becomes fragile. When love is measured by whether our needs are met, it becomes conditional. And when love is grounded in fairness, it crumbles under the weight of human imperfection.

> *But what if love is something else entirely?*

What if love is not a feeling to receive, but a commitment to give? What if fairness isn't the standard, and fulfillment isn't the goal? What if the real battlefield is not between you and your spouse—but within your own heart?

That's the uncomfortable but transformational premise of this book. Your marriage cannot heal until your perspective does. Before love can work, your **beliefs** about love, about marriage, and about yourself must be confronted and re-formed. Because real love—the kind that rebuilds broken covenants and restores wounded hearts—doesn't emerge from emotional convenience. It grows from inner clarity, humility, and conviction.

This kind of love isn't reactive—it's intentional. It doesn't wait for good behavior to bloom. It doesn't mirror what it receives. It initiates. It forgives. It endures. It isn't dependent on reciprocation. And perhaps the most radical thing about it is that it doesn't just come from us—it flows through us. It is fueled by something far greater than human will or mutual benefit.

As we'll explore more deeply in later chapters, the biblical term for this kind of love is *agape*. Unlike romantic love (*eros*) or friendship love (*philia*), agape is self-sacrificial, unconditional, and *covenantal*—a covenant; a committed, binding promise between two people and God, meant to be lasting, faithful, and based on mutual responsibility—not just a contract, but a sacred bond.. It is how the love God demonstrates toward us. It is the love Jesus embodied when He laid down His life. It is how God intended for marriage to be applied. And it is the only kind of love strong enough to resurrect a dying marriage.

Agape doesn't mean being passive or permissive. It means being principled and powerful in the way Christ was—strong enough to suffer, humble enough to serve, and secure enough to love without demanding control. It's not where most of us begin. But it is where we must aim, because anything less will crumble under the weight of real life.

Why You Must Go First

The Power Convictions presented in this book are not about making your spouse see the light. They are not weapons of manipulation or strategies to "fix" your partner. They are about reorienting *you* toward truth, humility, and change. They are about choosing to become a safe, stable, Spirit-led person even in the presence of an unsafe, unstable, or emotionally distant spouse.

This is not weakness. It is the deepest kind of strength. It is the strength of Christ in the Garden, choosing surrender over escape. It is the strength of forgiveness that absorbs pain instead of returning it. It is the strength of endurance that refuses to give in to bitterness, even when the path forward is steep and lonely.

If that sounds overwhelming, it's because it is—but only if you try to do it alone. Don't confuse the call to love first with carrying the weight alone. Grace meets you here—in the strain, in the sacrifice.

And yes, it feels unfair. But love has always been unfair. Grace is unfair. Mercy is unfair. And yet, this is the exact posture Christ took toward us: *"While we were still sinners, Christ died for us."* (Romans 5:8) He didn't wait for us to deserve His love. He didn't wait for us to apologize perfectly. He went first. And that's what makes it love.

To love someone who doesn't deserve it is to walk in the footsteps of your Savior. To lay down your need to win, to be right, to get even—that is where redemption begins. And if you don't start there, nothing else you try will last. You can't build intimacy on top of resentment. You can't grow connection while nurturing contempt. Someone has to stop the cycle. Someone has to lead the way. And in this moment, God might be asking that someone to be you.

A Word to the Wounded

Let me be clear: This is not a book that tells you to stay in abuse, pretend everything is fine, or erase healthy boundaries. If you are in danger, please seek safety. If your spouse is abusive, addicted, or chronically unrepentant, then your primary calling is to protect your wellbeing and pursue biblical counsel.

> ***Love never requires you to enable destruction or subject yourself to harm.***

But if you're simply stuck—discouraged, bitter, numb, or exhausted—then this book is for you. It is for the spouse who keeps showing up, trying harder, and wondering if anything will ever change. It is for the man or woman who wants to love well, but feels like they are doing it alone. It is for the one who has cried out to God with everything from whispers to wails, wondering, *"How long, Lord?"*

You are seen. You are not crazy. And you are not wasting your effort. Even if your spouse never changes, your heart can. Even if the marriage remains hard, your soul can find peace, maturity, and joy in Christ.

What to Expect in These Pages

This book presents four ***Power Conviction***—four cognitive shifts that must take place in your thinking *before* agape love can heal your marriage. They are hard, but holy. They are uncomfortable, but transformational. These are not just ideas to believe; they are truths to practice, wrestle with, and allow the Holy Spirit to engrave on your heart. Once you embrace them, you'll find that the six marriage-building principles that follow (in the companion book, *Re-Friending Your Marriage*) can finally take root and bear fruit.

You can't grow real love on rotten soil. So we're going to till the ground, pull up the weeds, and get your soul ready to love in a way that reflects Christ—whether your spouse joins you or not. Because in God's economy, faithfulness is never wasted. Obedience always matters.

> ***And love—real love, agape love—is never in vain.***

Are you ready to begin?

Chapter 1:
The Theology of Agape

Meet our Couple

They arrived early but already worn out. Body language stiff, eyes distant, every sentence wrapped in hurt and blame. She said, "I'm tired of doing everything alone." He replied, "And I'm tired of always being wrong." They didn't want to save their marriage. Not really. They wanted a referee. Someone to declare a winner.

As we talked, it became clear that both of them were convinced they were the one carrying the load. "I do everything," she said. "He doesn't care anymore." He shook his head, "I try. I try hard. But nothing is ever good enough for her."

They couldn't see each other. They couldn't even see themselves clearly. What they did see—loudly and painfully—was everything that wasn't working. They were exhausted from repeating the same arguments and confused about why love had become so complicated.

When I asked them what they wanted from counseling, they both said, "I just want things to change." But as they described the change they hoped for, it always started with what the other person needed to do differently.

What they didn't know was that real healing would begin—not when one of them changed first—but when each laid down their weapons, looked inward, and started owning their own mindset, actions, and character.

> *This chapter opens with their frustration, but it ends with a deeper truth: they have more power than they think—not over each other, but over themselves.*
>
> *They had come in hoping I would fix their marriage. But the work ahead would be far more personal.*

Welcome to the journey.

This book begins with that truth, and walks step by step through the process of becoming a person who can love well, regardless of what your spouse does. And it starts by shifting the focus from fairness to faithfulness, from blame to responsibility, and from being right to becoming righteous.

When we talk about love in our culture, we almost always mean something that fluctuates, something that responds to how we feel or how others behave. We say, "I love you," and what we often mean is, "I enjoy you," or, "I feel something good toward you right now." But in marriage, if love is only a mood or a response, it will collapse the first time it's tested. And it will be tested.

God never intended love to be a reward for good behavior. In fact, biblical love often begins where human affection ends. This chapter is about reframing your understanding of love by looking at it theologically—through God's eyes, not just your own. Because until you understand love the way God defines it, you will keep trying to build your marriage on something too soft to last.

Love as God's Nature

Scripture does not merely say that God is loving. It says that God *is* love (1 John 4:8). That means love isn't just something God does; it's who He is. And the kind of love God demonstrates is called *agape*—a selfless, sacrificial, unbreakable love. It is the kind of love that doesn't depend on the worthiness of the recipient but flows out of the unchanging character of the Giver. In 1 Corinthians 13, verse 4 God declares "love is patient, love is kind…" (NIV). It goes on to fully describe love in action and outcomes. But these two sum up the whole. If one is patient and kind first, the rest will naturally follow, because the focus is not on selfishness, but on the object of one's love, the other person.

Agape love is what moved God to create us, knowing we would rebel. It's what sent Jesus to the cross while we were still sinners. It's what keeps the Holy Spirit pursuing us even when we're resistant or rebellious. Agape love is the posture of a holy God toward a hurting world. And it's the model He gives us for loving each other—especially in marriage.

The World's Love vs. God's Love

The love we see in movies and social media is usually based on mutual benefit. It's built on chemistry, compatibility, and convenience. When it stops feeling good, we assume something must be wrong. But God's love doesn't work that way. God's love isn't about emotion—it's about covenant. It's not sustained by attraction but by decision. And it's not validated by how it feels, but by how it endures.

This is not to say emotions don't matter—they do. Emotional connection, affection, and delight are wonderful gifts in marriage. But when we treat those things as the foundation of love instead of the fruit of love, we invert the entire structure. Agape puts obedience before affection, and in doing so, it often revives affection where it was dying.

Agape in Marriage: Why It's the Goal

When couples come into counseling, they often say things like, "We've fallen out of love," or "I just don't feel anything anymore." But agape doesn't ask, "Do I feel love?" It asks, "Am I willing to give love?" That one question changes everything.

> *Am I willing to give love?*

Agape is the only kind of love that can survive the storms of marriage. It stays when things are hard. It speaks kindly when it would be easier to lash out. It forgives when resentment feels justified. It doesn't erase boundaries or overlook sin, but it moves toward the other person with grace and truth.

When Paul wrote 1 Corinthians 13, he wasn't giving advice for a wedding ceremony. He was describing the kind of love required in a community of broken people trying to live as the body of Christ. Every descriptor of love in that passage—patient, kind, not rude, not self-seeking—is a picture of what it takes to love someone who doesn't make it easy.

That's why agape isn't natural. It's supernatural. It's the love God gives us—and the love He invites us to pass on, not because the other person has earned it, but because we've been transformed by it ourselves.

A Love That Starts With God and Returns to God

The only reason we can give this kind of love is because we've received it. John tells us, "We love because He first loved us" (1 John 4:19, NIV). That's not just a poetic phrase—it's a theological reality. The capacity to love in a godly way is not manufactured by willpower; it is rooted in our relationship with the God who *is* love. If your soul is disconnected from the source, your heart will eventually run dry.

That's why agape love must begin vertically before it flows horizontally. Your spouse is not the source of love in your life—God is. Your spouse may block it, reject it, or fail to return it, but they cannot stop you from receiving love from God and choosing to live in it.

This doesn't make the pain of rejection or disappointment disappear, but it transforms the way you respond. Instead of using your spouse's failures as permission to withdraw, you begin seeing them as an opportunity to reflect Christ. Instead of waiting to be loved before you act in love, you live from the love you already possess.

Agape and the Cross

No picture of agape is more vivid than the cross of Christ. Jesus didn't die because we were lovable. He died because He is love. He absorbed the wrath we deserved. He bore the shame we couldn't carry. He opened a door we could never unlock on our own.

That is the kind of love God calls you to bring into your marriage. Not because your spouse has earned it, but because Christ has already demonstrated it. And the more you embrace that reality, the less you'll find yourself needing to control, punish, or manipulate your spouse to get what you think you need.

Agape is not easy. It is not instant. But it is powerful. It is healing. It is redemptive. And it is possible—because it doesn't come from you. It comes from the God who loved you first and loves you still.

Living Out Agape: The Invitation

So how do you begin? You start by acknowledging that your view of love may have been more shaped by culture than by Christ. You begin by letting the Spirit of God convict you—not just about your actions, but about your assumptions. You open your heart to the possibility that you may have been measuring love in the wrong units.

Then you choose. You choose to stop reacting and start becoming. You choose to surrender the scoreboard. You choose to release the demand for fairness and embrace the call to faithfulness. You choose to love not because it's fair, but because it's Christlike.

You won't do it perfectly. You'll struggle. You'll slip. But as you commit to live this kind of love, you will begin to taste its freedom. You'll stop being enslaved to your spouse's behavior. You'll stop waiting for things to change before you find peace. You'll begin to reflect the character of Christ in your home, and that alone is a miracle in the making.

Agape is not the starting point of most marriages. But it must become the goal. Because anything less will fail. And everything more begins here.

Chapter 2:
The Psychology of the Wounded Self

They sat on opposite ends of the couch, each folding their arms like armor.

"I just don't feel loved anymore," she said, her voice cracking under the weight of weeks of silence.

"And I feel like no matter what I do, it's never enough," he replied, eyes down, tone clipped.

This wasn't a new conversation. In fact, it was the third version of it that week. But they kept coming back to it because something about it felt unresolved—unfinished, unsatisfying.

As I listened, it became clear that both of them were reacting to their feelings as if they were hard facts. Her loneliness convinced her she was unloved. His shame convinced him he was a failure. Neither accusation was completely true—but neither was completely false either. The real issue was that their emotions had become the judge and jury for their marriage.

"I just want to feel better," she said.

"I just want to stop feeling like the bad guy," he responded.

So we paused the discussion. I asked them to describe their inner dialogue—the stories they were telling themselves. And for the first time, they realized they were interpreting their spouse's actions entirely through the lens of their personal pain.

This may be hard to hear, especially if your pain feels raw or recent. But pain, when acknowledged with honesty, can become one of God's most honest teachers.

And as painful as those feelings were, they were only signals. Not conclusions. Not ultimate truth. Just emotional cues pointing toward deeper issues waiting to be discovered—together.

The Problem with How We Love

Before a person can love with the self-giving depth of agape, they must confront the barriers within themselves that block that kind of love. No one grows up unscathed. Our capacity to love and be loved is shaped early by our experiences of acceptance, rejection, belonging, discipline, and emotional safety. And when those foundations are cracked or missing, our adult relationships suffer—even when our intentions are good.

This chapter explores how emotional wounds—especially those left unhealed—create distortions in our sense of self and hinder our ability to love well. We'll look at the impact of shame, unresolved grief, unmet needs, and protective false beliefs. If agape is the goal, this is the work of clearing the rubble to make space for it to take root.

We Love From Who We Are

Every spouse brings a story into the marriage. Not just a history of where they've been, but a narrative about who they are, how relationships work, and what love means. These narratives are often formed in childhood and shaped by key relationships: parents, caretakers, siblings, teachers, and early peers.

When a child grows up in an emotionally safe environment, they learn that they have worth, that their needs matter, and that love is dependable. But when those experiences are marred by neglect, inconsistency, criticism, or abandonment, the child often learns something very different: "I am not enough," or "Love is earned," or "Closeness is dangerous."

When parents don't provide stable boundaries, affirmations, and healthy feedback, or worse yet, when they move the goal posts through conditional love messages, children fail to establish a true sense of self. This creates an instability called an *arrested* development, a state where the child is dependent on outside sources to know who they are and how to feel. The result is an inability to feel safe, to know and trust love in the truest sense, and to seek appropriate affirmations. They learn to pursue approval or test all relationships, fearing disappointment and betrayal at the slightest hint of failure.

These wounds don't stay in childhood. They come with us into marriage. And without awareness, we end up relating to our spouse not as they are—but through the lens of our past.

Shame and the Fragile Self

One of the most powerful forces blocking agape love is shame. Not guilt, which says, "I did something wrong," but shame, which says, "There is something wrong with me." Shame doesn't stay quiet. It whispers in every moment of conflict, every failed attempt at closeness, every feeling of rejection: *See? You're not lovable. You're too much. You'll never get this right.*

Before we look at Scripture, let's take a breath. If shame feels like a familiar voice in your life, you're not alone—and the Bible has much to say to that ache.

Shame came into the world at the beginning, when Adam and Eve fell from grace, after eating the forbidden fruit. We see it active in their realization that they are *naked*, and are hiding themselves with aprons of leaves. This is more than a physical shame. This is a realization that they are no longer acceptable in themselves. Up until then, they were without blame, but now, they were unacceptable due to the sin they brought into their lives. Shame attaches to us all from our actions. It takes our bad actions, and then defines us as bad actors. Human being have been hiding their shame since that fateful day in the garden, out of fear of rejection, abandonment, and judgment.

When shame drives a person's self-perception, they become overly reactive in relationships. They either withdraw to protect themselves from further wounding or lash out to preemptively defend against perceived threats. Even in moments of calm, shame filters love through suspicion. A compliment feels manipulative. An act of kindness seems conditional. Real intimacy is always just out of reach.

Shame makes love feel dangerous. And until it is named and healed, it will sabotage the very connection we long for.

The Armor of False Beliefs

To survive in a world where love has been inconsistent or painful, people build protective beliefs. These beliefs start as coping strategies but harden into convictions over time:

- "People will leave if I'm honest."

- "I must be perfect to be accepted."
- "Needing others is weak."
- "If I don't control things, I'll be hurt."

While these beliefs may have served a purpose in a chaotic or untrustworthy environment, they are devastating in a marriage. They prevent vulnerability. They stifle empathy. They turn partnership into performance.

The tragic irony is that many spouses live behind these defenses without realizing it. They long for connection, but their inner programming is built for protection. Love gets blocked not because they don't want to give it, but because they're still trying to survive a war that ended years ago.

Unmet Needs and the Search for Substitutes

Every human being carries legitimate needs—attachment, affirmation, emotional regulation, physical safety, significance. But when these needs go unmet, we don't stop needing—we just start compensating. We look for substitutes. Some people try to meet their emotional needs through overachievement. Others turn to substances, sexuality, ministry, people-pleasing, or control. These strategies offer temporary relief but create long-term distortion.

The void in the soul from unmet needs creates a vacuum. Like a black hole it tries to suck in love from anyone or anything nearby. We call this an attachment disorder, but really it is an unmet need for connection that one can trust. Individuals in this plight tend to aggressively pull and draw too hard on the resources of others because they are fundamentally too needy and not at all self-aware, or, if confronted with their behavior, have a strong belief that they have no choice because they need love and no one is giving it to them if they don't grasp for it.

When a spouse tries to get from marriage what only God or early nurturing should have provided, they place impossible pressure on the relationship. The marriage becomes less about loving the other person and more about extracting from them the security or validation that was missing long before. The spouse becomes a surrogate parent, therapist, or savior—roles they were never designed to carry.

Emotional Fusion and the Loss of Boundaries

Another danger for the wounded self is emotional fusion—the inability to separate one's own emotions from another's. A person with poor boundaries may feel responsible for their spouse's moods, behavior, or spiritual condition. They might swing between guilt and resentment, constantly asking, *"Am I doing enough?"* or *"What else can I fix?"*

What you may be feeling in your marriage is not new. In fact, it's often a pattern rooted far earlier than either of you realize. This dynamic often emerges from family systems where roles were blurred or children had to parent their parents. Without healing, these patterns continue in marriage, where one spouse becomes over-functioning and the other under-functioning. True agape can't grow in this imbalance because it's not rooted in freedom—it's rooted in fear and control. If you've seen yourself in these patterns, don't despair. The fact that you can name it is the beginning of changing it.

From Surviving to Healing

Healing begins with awareness. You cannot change what you will not name. If your wounds are driving your relational style, your first act of love might not be directed toward your spouse—but toward yourself. Not in selfishness, but in honesty.

- What beliefs about yourself are you carrying into the marriage?
- Where did you first learn what love means?
- What are you trying to get from your spouse that only God can give?

Bringing these questions to God in prayer, journaling, and sometimes counseling is the beginning of reclaiming a healthy self. As you grow in identity, security, and clarity, your capacity to love—freely, without manipulation or neediness—will grow too.

Why This Work Matters

You cannot give what you do not possess. And you cannot fully possess love until you believe you are already loved. The wounded self makes love transactional: *If I do enough, I'll be loved.* But the healed self begins with this truth: *Because I am loved, I can now love without fear.*

You may still wrestle with this truth—but you are not disqualified by that struggle. You are already on the path. This is the kind of selfhood agape requires—not perfection, but rootedness. Not achievement, but identity. A heart grounded in grace, secure in Christ, no longer driven by the ghosts of its past.

> ***This is the soil in which agape can grow.***

Let's keep digging.

Chapter 3:
The Culture of Self Before Sacrifice

She sat in silence while he vented. Not because she agreed, but because she had stopped trying to defend herself. "I can't win with you," he said. "Whatever I feel, you tell me I shouldn't feel it."

She answered softly, "Because your feelings aren't the only truth."

That session marked a shift—not because they resolved anything, but because they finally admitted that their emotions had become both weapon and compass. He felt unloved, so he assumed she was unloving. She felt overwhelmed, so she assumed he was unreliable. Both were reacting to their own experience as if it defined reality.

I asked them a question I often pose: "What's more important—how you feel, or what is actually true?"

It wasn't a dismissal of their emotions. It was an invitation to explore what those emotions were pointing to. Because when we treat feelings as facts, we stop growing. But when we treat them as signals, we gain insight.

This couple began to shift—not all at once, but gradually. They started asking better questions. They learned to say, "I'm feeling angry, but that doesn't necessarily mean you're wrong," or "I'm feeling scared—help me understand what's happening."

> *They stopped using emotions as evidence. They started using them as entry points.*

And that made all the difference.

When Feelings Replace Facts

Our modern world teaches us to prioritize self over everything else. "Follow your heart," "Do what makes you happy," and "You deserve better" are not just slogans—they're mantras baked into the cultural air we breathe. We are trained to elevate personal fulfillment as the highest good and view anything that threatens our comfort or self-expression as toxic. Unfortunately, this worldview does not prepare us to love well. In fact, it sets us up to fail at love altogether.

Love, especially agape love, doesn't begin with self-gratification. It begins with self-giving. And when a culture idolizes the self, sacrifice feels like oppression, patience feels like weakness, and forgiveness feels like self-betrayal. This chapter explores how the culture of self distorts our expectations of marriage and prevents us from embracing the kind of love that heals.

The Rise of the Therapeutic Gospel

In the past, people viewed personal growth through the lens of virtue—becoming more honest, courageous, disciplined, and humble. Today, we view growth in terms of emotional wellness and personal empowerment. We no longer ask, "Am I becoming good?" We ask, "Am I feeling better?"

This shift has birthed what some theologians and counselors call the *therapeutic gospel*[1]—a version of Christianity that centers not on the holiness of God and the transformation of the soul, but on emotional validation and the relief of discomfort. In this gospel, God exists to help us feel better about ourselves. Sin is rebranded as trauma, conviction is mistaken for shame, and moral formation is replaced by self-discovery.

While emotional health matters, emotional comfort is not the same as healing. The therapeutic gospel avoids the cross. It offers empathy without accountability, support without sanctification. It treats feelings as facts and resists any call to deny the self in order to grow. And in doing so, it creates fragile disciples—and fragile marriages.

When Feelings Become Sovereign

We live in a time when feelings have become the highest authority. If I feel hurt, then someone must have harmed me. If I feel unloved, then my partner must be unloving. If I feel unhappy, then something must be wrong with my circumstances or my spouse. But Scripture teaches us that feelings, while real, are not always reliable. The heart is deceitful (Jeremiah 17:9), and our emotions often reflect wounds, fears, and lies—not reality.

When feelings become sovereign, truth becomes negotiable. We begin to evaluate our marriages not by covenant standards but by our moment-to-moment emotional

---

[1] The term "therapeutic gospel" is used in the spirit of critique found in the writings of David Powlison (CCEF), referring to a view of God oriented toward emotional comfort over spiritual sanctification.

temperature. We stop asking, "Is this holy?" and start asking, "Is this enjoyable?" We stop committing to what is right and start chasing what feels good. And over time, we begin to resent anything—or anyone—that asks us to sacrifice, persevere, or grow up.

Feelings vs. Covenant: The Battle Beneath the Surface

Nowhere is the clash between modern thinking and biblical love more evident than in the conflict between feelings and covenant. In today's culture, how we feel is treated as the compass that should guide every decision. This is especially true in marriage. If you feel disconnected, it must mean something is broken. If you feel bored, it must mean the spark is gone. If you feel frustrated, it must mean your spouse is failing you.

But covenant doesn't function that way. Covenant is not built on feelings—it's built on promises. It is a sacred commitment to act in love, regardless of the current emotional climate. In Scripture, covenant love is what holds God to His people even when they rebel, wander, or betray Him. It is a binding agreement, not a mutual mood.

When we elevate feelings over covenant, we end up submitting our vows to our emotions. "For better or worse" becomes "for better or until I'm unhappy." But feelings are like weather—they change. They can be influenced by hormones, sleep, stress, or even what we had for breakfast. They are poor captains for the ship of marriage.

That's not to say feelings don't matter. God created emotions, and they are meant to signal important truths. But they are indicators, not dictators. A covenant-centered marriage respects feelings but isn't ruled by them. It acknowledges emotional pain, confusion, or distance while still holding fast to the deeper commitment: *I am for you, and I am not leaving.*

This is where true love becomes powerful. But to make that shift, we must first understand what feelings are—and what they are not. Feelings are not facts, but neither are they irrelevant. They are like the check engine light in your car: they alert you that something under the hood needs attention, but they don't tell you exactly what the problem is or how to fix it.

> ***Covenant is not built on feelings—it's built on promises: I am for you, and I am not leaving.***

Think of emotions like a code reader a mechanic uses to diagnose a car. When the dash light comes on, a code provides a clue about the system that needs inspection. But reading the code doesn't repair the engine. The code isn't the issue itself—it's a signal. Likewise, your feelings are signals. They point toward deeper issues—disappointments, unmet needs, false expectations, internal wounds—but they are not the issue itself.

When we elevate feelings to the status of truth, we mistake the alert for the engine. We start treating the symptom as the substance. But when we recognize feelings as indicators of content rather than content themselves, we gain the clarity to ask better questions: What is this emotion *pointing to*? Is this about now—or about something old surfacing? Where am I out of sync with my covenant, or where might my spouse be disconnected from theirs?

A covenant view of love listens to feelings without letting them steer the ship. It uses emotion to diagnose, not to dictate. And in that space—where feelings are respected but not enthroned—real healing begins. That's when love matures. It becomes durable. And in that durability, trust is born.

> **A covenant view of love listens to feelings without letting them steer the ship.**

The Idol of Self-Fulfillment

Marriage was never meant to fulfill you. That may sound disappointing, even offensive, to modern ears. But biblically, the purpose of marriage is not to complete you—it is to *refine* you. It is a covenant relationship designed not to make you *happy*, but to make you *holy*. Joy is a byproduct, not a guarantee.

When we treat marriage as a tool for self-fulfillment, we make our spouse responsible for our internal well-being. We turn covenant into contract: *You give me what I need, and I'll stay.* But when they fail to meet our expectations—as all humans eventually do—we begin to justify resentment, emotional withdrawal, or even escape.

Agape love challenges this entirely. It does not ask, "What am I getting?" but "What am I giving?" It shifts the purpose of marriage from consumerism to discipleship. It invites us to become the kind of people who can love like Christ, not because we are being perfectly loved, but because we are being inwardly transformed.

When marriage becomes a mirror for self-fulfillment, our spouse stops being a partner and starts being a project. We begin to focus more on how they need to change than how we are being called to love. And when they disappoint us—which they will—we begin to doubt the value of the marriage itself.

But agape flips that entirely. It reminds us that the goal of marriage is not to find someone who meets all our needs, but to become someone who reflects God's love even when our needs aren't fully met. Agape teaches us that love doesn't require ideal circumstances; it requires a transformed heart.

This kind of love requires dying to self. It means surrendering the illusion that life—and love—exist to serve our preferences. It means trading entitlement for endurance, comfort for commitment, validation for virtue. It's the kind of love that survives betrayal, boredom, and broken expectations. Not because it ignores pain, but because it answers pain with faithfulness.

Choosing Sacrifice in a Culture of Self

To live this kind of love is to swim upstream. It will feel unnatural. You'll be misunderstood. You'll be tempted to believe you're being taken advantage of. But if your model is Christ—not culture—then you'll see that love always costs something. The cross was not convenient. The gospel was not cheap. And real marriage never flourishes when one or both partners are chasing ease.

So where do we begin? We start by naming the cultural lies that have shaped our expectations. We admit that we have sometimes worshipped comfort more than character. We confess that we've confused our feelings with truth. And then—we choose. We choose to make covenant the anchor. We choose to treat emotion as information, not instruction. We choose to sacrifice not because it's easy, but because it's holy.

In a culture of self, love that lasts will look like rebellion. So, let's be rebels in the right direction.

Chapter 4:
Asking the Right Question

He sat across from me on the couch, arms folded, lips tight. His wife had just finished recounting—through tears—the slow unraveling of their marriage. She talked about the distance, the lack of warmth, the constant deflection of responsibility. When she finished, I turned gently to him and asked, "What's going on inside you right now?"

He shrugged. "I just don't get it. I'm not doing anything wrong. Why is she so unhappy?"

He shifted in his seat, scanning the room for support that wouldn't come. His voice grew sharper. "I mean, if I'm not yelling, if I'm paying the bills, what else does she want?"
She flinched. Her hands trembled slightly in her lap. "You never ask me how I feel. You don't seem to care about what I carry. You just… manage me."
I paused, letting the silence settle, then asked again, "What's going on inside you when she says that?"
This time, his eyes filled—not with tears, but with confusion. "I feel like I'm failing. But I don't know how to do it differently."

There it was—the wrong question. Subtly defensive, quietly self-exonerating. It assumed innocence, placed blame, and closed the door to deeper understanding.

What he really needed to ask was something far less comfortable: What has she been experiencing from me that I've refused to see? That question—if he had the courage to ask it—would not only have led him to truth, but possibly to healing.

We've all done it.

Something goes wrong in a relationship. Someone lets us down. A promise is broken. Our heart feels bruised or betrayed. And what do we instinctively do? We ask a question. But not just any question. We ask *our* question—the one that feels natural, justifiable, emotionally obvious. Something like:

- Why do people always take advantage of me?
- Why can't my spouse just see how hard I try?
- What's wrong with *them*?

And here's the tragic irony: the answer to these kinds of questions almost never helps. In fact, they usually hurt.

When you ask the *wrong* question, whatever answer you get will likely reinforce your frustration, fuel your bitterness, or justify your retreat. The problem isn't that you don't get an answer. It's that you get the *wrong* answer—because the question itself was loaded with blame, self-justification, or fear.

> **The quality of your question determines the direction of your growth.**

Wrong questions lead us deeper into confusion, because they arise from a place of wounded pride or emotional reaction, not from wisdom. And if your convictions are being shaped by emotionally reactive questions, your conclusions will be unstable, and your direction unreliable.

This chapter is an invitation to pause before you speak, to think before you ask, and to learn how to frame the *right* question—the kind that opens the door to insight, healing, and growth.

The Trap of the Wrong Question

Wrong questions feel right in the moment. That's why they're so dangerous. They align with our pain, our insecurity, or our need to be right. They act like emotional echo chambers, giving voice to what we already believe and amplifying it.

Consider a man who, after an argument with his wife, asks, "Why does she always overreact?" That question assumes the problem is entirely hers. It invites him to become defensive and dismissive rather than curious and repentant. Or think of the woman who, after years of disappointment, asks herself, "Why did I ever think I could be loved?" That question reinforces despair and shuts the door on hope.

Wrong questions are seductive because they validate what we already feel. But feelings, as we've already seen, are not always faithful guides. The question is not whether a feeling is real—of course it is. The question is whether it leads to truth.

"A fool hath no delight in understanding, but that his heart may discover itself." — Proverbs 18:2

If all you want is confirmation, any question will do. But if you want convictional clarity, you must learn to ask a better question.

Why Wrong Questions Harm

Wrong questions don't just mislead. They *harm*. They shut down learning. They escalate conflict. They deepen victimhood.

Here's why:

1. **They reinforce bias.** Wrong questions aren't neutral. They're already slanted toward a preferred outcome—one that lets us off the hook or paints others in the worst light.

2. **They blind us to our part.** A self-justifying question rarely includes the possibility that I may be the one in need of correction.

3. **They stall progress.** If I'm asking how to escape responsibility instead of how to mature through it, I'll stay stuck.

4. **They damage relationships.** When your internal narrative is built on accusatory or despairing questions, it becomes the lens through which you see others.

This is especially true in marriage. A question like, "Why can't they change?" builds resentment. A better question might be, "What in me resists loving them where they are?"

We see this dynamic in Scripture too. After Cain's offering is rejected, God asks him a *better* question: "Why are you angry?" (Genesis 4:6). But Cain avoids that question, and instead asks himself a worse one: "How do I get rid of my brother?" The result is tragic.

Wrong questions don't just lead to bad answers. They lead to destructive actions.

Throughout Scripture, questions are used not merely to extract information—but to expose the heart. When God asked Adam, *"Where are you?"* (Gen. 3:9), it wasn't because He didn't know. It was because Adam needed to recognize his own disconnection. When Jesus asked the disciples, *"Who do you say I am?"* He was not gathering data. He was leading them to a moment of confession and clarity.

> *"Who do you say I am?"*

Right questions are divine tools. They lead not just to answers—but to repentance, insight, and intimacy. Learning to ask better questions is a spiritual discipline, not just a psychological strategy.

The Right Question Opens the Door

If the wrong question locks the door to growth, the right question is the key that opens it.

Right questions are uncomfortable. They challenge our assumptions. They shift the spotlight from others onto ourselves. But they also invite truth, clarity, and healing.

A wife frustrated over her husband's emotional withdrawal might ask, *"Why does he shut down every time we talk?"*
A better question would be, *"Have I created a space where he feels safe enough to open up?"*

Likewise, a husband weary of emotional disconnection might ask, *"Why doesn't she appreciate anything I do?"*

A better question might be, *"What kind of connection is she longing for that I might be missing?"*

Instead of:

Why don't they respect me?

Ask:

What have I done that might have made respect difficult?

Instead of:

What's wrong with them?

Ask:

What might I not understand about their struggle?

Instead of:

How do I prove I'm right?

Ask:

What do I need to own in this?

The right question doesn't feel emotionally satisfying at first. It feels costly. But it leads you toward a better future.

"If any of you lack wisdom, let him ask of God... and it shall be given him." — James 1:5

> ***Right questions yield answers you can build a life on.***

How to Ask Better Questions

Start by pausing. Most of our bad questions are born in the moment of emotional reaction. Don't trust your first question. Let it pass through a filter:

1. **STOP** — Am I trying to win, avoid, or deflect?
2. **THINK** — What would a humble, truth-seeking person ask here?
3. **ASK** — What question leads me toward responsibility and wisdom?

Jesus was a master of questions. He rarely offered quick answers. Instead, He asked: "Who do you say I am?" or "What do you want me to do for you?" or "Do you want to be well?"

These questions weren't rhetorical. They were revealing. They helped people uncover what they actually needed—not just what they thought they wanted.

Convictional living means learning to ask questions that align with truth rather than emotion.

What Are You Really Asking?

Every day you ask questions—internally, silently, emotionally. Some of them shape how you see yourself. Others shape how you treat others. All of them shape your direction.

So ask yourself:

- *What question have I been asking that keeps me stuck?*
- *What question have I avoided because the answer might convict me?*

The wrong question protects your ego. The right question purifies your path.

Which one are you asking?

When the Question Shifts to the Right Question

> Jason came into counseling convinced he was doing everything right. "I work hard. I come home. I don't cheat or drink. What else does she want from me?" he asked, arms crossed, tone defensive. Marla sat beside him, exhausted. "I just want to feel like I matter to him," she whispered.
>
> For weeks, Jason kept **asking the same question**: Why is she always so unhappy? But that question only made him more resentful and more confused. One day, I challenged him: "Jason, what question do you **not** want to ask right now?"
>
> He looked at me for a long time. Then said, quietly, "What is it like to be married to me?"
>
> That was the moment things began to shift. Jason didn't love the answers he heard—but they softened him. And for the first time, Marla didn't feel dismissed. She felt seen.
>
> He started asking new questions after that—better questions. He stopped trying to prove he was a good husband and started learning how to become one. And slowly, the tension in the room gave way to tenderness. Not because she changed, but because he asked the right question—and let it change him.

Now, before we turn the page, pause and reflect. What question has been driving the way you see your marriage? What internal script keeps playing when things go wrong? The questions we ask in quiet moments shape the direction of our growth—or our stagnation. Don't let pain, pride, or fear frame your inquiries. Instead, ask like someone who wants to grow. Ask like someone who believes God still speaks. Ask like someone who knows healing starts with humility. Because the right question, asked in the presence of God, can open the door to clarity, conviction, and change. And that may be the very breakthrough your heart—and your marriage—has been waiting for.

In the next chapter, we'll take another step forward—moving from the questions we ask to the truths we must face when the answers come. Because when conviction starts to form, so does the cost. And clarity always comes with responsibility.

PART TWO

The Power Convictions

Transformation requires truth. This section introduces my four ***Power Convictions***—biblical, actionable principles that guide your choices in the face of pain, conflict, and betrayal. These convictions reposition your heart from reaction to responsibility, helping you love well even when it's not reciprocated.

Chapter 5:
I Must Challenge My False Beliefs

She believed: "Marriage should be 50/50."

He believed: "She should know what I need without me having to say it."

One evening, they came in with a list—each had written down what they expected marriage to be. His list included things like "respect," "peace," "regular intimacy." Hers had "emotional safety," "shared goals," "spiritual leadership."

I looked at both lists and asked, "Where did these expectations come from?"

They stared at me blankly. "Isn't this what a marriage should look like?" she asked. "Isn't this normal?" he added.

But what they believed was normal had been inherited from their families, shaped by media, distorted by pain. And much of it was unexamined. She was holding him to standards she never explained. He was punishing her for failing assumptions he never questioned.

When they began unpacking where their beliefs came from, they discovered that many of their assumptions weren't shared, weren't healthy, and weren't leading them toward unity.

They agreed to write a new list together—not of expectations, but of shared convictions. And for the first time, their marriage started to feel like a partnership instead of a standoff.

POWER CONVICTION #1:
Challenge your own beliefs about marriage in general, and about the current state of your marriage in particular.

Here's an example,

> *"Marriage is about two people working together. I will bring 50%, and he will bring 50% and we will get a whole marriage. He's not doing his part. Until he steps up, I am not going to do any more. It's on him to show me he's willing before I take on any more burden or risk."*

Neither one of these commonly held beliefs will heal or even hold your marriage together.

This is the first of the Four Power Convictions, and it cuts directly to the root of marital frustration: faulty assumptions. Many couples enter marriage with silent contracts—unspoken expectations about roles, fairness, effort, and what love should feel like. When those expectations are disappointed, resentment often replaces affection, and defense mechanisms take the place of vulnerability.

Every broken marriage is built on a foundation of broken beliefs. Not always dramatic or obvious ones—but subtle, quiet, deeply embedded assumptions that shape the way we see ourselves, our spouse, and the meaning of love. These beliefs are often inherited, reinforced by pain, and rarely questioned. But if they go unchallenged, they become the invisible architecture of relational failure.

This chapter is about courage. The courage to turn inward and ask *the right question*, "What am I believing that isn't true?" before asking, "What is my spouse doing that isn't right?" It is about taking full ownership of your thinking—not your spouse's behavior—as the starting place for change.

Because change that begins in your mindset can radically reshape your marriage, even before circumstances shift.

Belief Drives Behavior

We like to think our choices are driven by logic, faith, or moral values. But the truth is, most of our behaviors are driven by beliefs we don't consciously acknowledge. These beliefs are often rooted in childhood experiences, trauma, or long-standing relational patterns. Some beliefs are helpful and grounded in biblical truth. Others are false, distorted, and self-protective. For example:

- "Love means I should always feel happy."
- "If I'm not being treated fairly, I don't owe anything back."
- "My spouse should already know what I need."
- "If I show kindness first, I'll be taken advantage of."
- "If I forgive, I'm saying what they did was okay."
- "If I admit my fault, I'll lose all power."
- "If I lower my guard, I'll get hurt again."

These aren't just thoughts. They are operating systems. They shape how we speak, how we interpret conflict, how we justify behavior, and how we position ourselves in relationships. And often, we don't even know we're doing it.

The hard truth is that many of our most deeply held beliefs were formed in pain, not truth. They were shaped not in the presence of love, but in its absence. And while they may have helped us feel safe or in control, they sabotage intimacy.

Survival Thinking vs. Redemptive Thinking

Pain teaches. But what it teaches isn't always right. A child who learns that vulnerability leads to rejection will grow into an adult who equates openness with danger. A teenager who finds attention only through performance may become a spouse who believes love must be earned through perfection.

These survival beliefs are designed to protect us. They help us manage fear, prevent rejection, and avoid shame. But they also isolate us, control us, and distort our relationships.

In marriage, survival thinking shows up as defensiveness, emotional withdrawal, stonewalling, passive-aggression, hypercriticism, or controlling behavior. These aren't just relational sins—they are protective patterns. And behind every pattern is a belief: *I have to do this to survive.*

Redemptive thinking begins when we ask: *Is this belief helping me love well? Does this belief align with God's Word? Is this how Jesus would see my situation?*

> ***Is this belief helping me love well?***

Romans 12:2 exhorts us to be "transformed by the renewing of your mind." This isn't just about theological correctness—it's about reprogramming our emotional and relational instincts. It's choosing to think like someone who is beloved, secure, and called to give, not someone abandoned, afraid, or in constant debt.

All Behavior Has a Purpose

One of the most important shifts in both counseling and marriage is understanding this: *All behavior has a purpose*[2]. Even behavior that seems irrational, reckless, or selfish is usually attempting to meet some need—often a need the person can't articulate.

Alfred Adler and his successors, including Rudolf Dreikurs and Don Dinkmeyer, emphasized that misbehavior is a form of mistaken strategy. Beneath the action is a longing for significance, belonging, affirmation, or connection. The behavior may be unhealthy, but the need is real.

In marriage, that means the anger, coldness, reactivity, or avoidance that drives us apart is often a clumsy cry for closeness. Beneath the sarcasm may be shame. Beneath the silence may be fear. Behind the control may be desperation to feel safe.

This is especially true when emotions are dysregulated. When your spouse yells, avoids you, or withdraws, the behavior might seem disrespectful or uncaring—but it might actually be fear in disguise. It might be an internal message like, *If I speak, I'll be misunderstood.* Or, *If I engage, I'll fail.* Or, *If I'm fully seen, I'll be rejected.*

Fear, Shame, and the Longing for Connection

At the heart of most false beliefs is fear—specifically, the fear of being unworthy of love. This fear creates shame, which then drives behavior. The more shame we carry, the

---

[2] Based on the classical Adlerian framework of purposeful behavior as developed by Alfred Adler, Rudolf Dreikurs, and Don Dinkmeyer.

more we hide. The more we hide, the more disconnected we become.

Scripture shows us this clearly in the story of Adam and Eve. After they sinned, "they realized they were naked; so they sewed fig leaves together and made coverings for themselves. Then the man and his wife heard the sound of the Lord God… and they hid" (Genesis 3:7-8, NIV). They hid because they believed they were unacceptable. Their behavior—hiding and blaming—was driven by shame.

That pattern continues today. We long for intimacy, but we fear exposure. We want to be seen and known, but we're afraid of being rejected when we are. So we build modern fig leaves—sarcasm, silence, control, perfectionism. We don't stop wanting connection; we just get better at hiding our need for it.

But God still comes walking in the garden. He still asks, "Where are you?" Not because He doesn't know—but because He wants us to come out of hiding. He invites us to bring our shame, our false beliefs, and our relational fig leaves into His presence so He can clothe us in truth.

> *"Where are you?"*

Replacing Lies with Truth

Challenging your false beliefs is not about self-shaming. It's about honesty. It's about having the courage to say, *Maybe I've been seeing this wrong.* Maybe what I've assumed about myself, my spouse, or love itself needs to be unlearned.

Here are some examples:

Lie: "If I'm not treated well, I don't owe love."

Truth: "I can love because Christ first loved me—even when I didn't deserve it."

Lie: "If I show weakness, I'll be crushed."

Truth: "My strength is made perfect in weakness."

Lie: "If I let my guard down, I'll be hurt again."

Truth: "Perfect love casts out fear."

These are not just theological corrections—they are heart recalibrations. They require repetition, prayer, and often counseling. But with time, these truths displace the lies that keep love shallow and reactive.

Asking the Right Questions

As you reflect on your beliefs, don't just ask what your spouse needs to change. Ask yourself:

What am I believing right now about love, fairness, or worthiness?

Where did I learn that belief?

Is it helping me love, or helping me hide?

Is it rooted in truth—or in pain?

This is the deeper work. It's not glamorous. It won't give you quick results. But it's the soil in which agape love can finally grow.

When you begin to challenge your false beliefs, you begin to take authority over your patterns. You stop being the victim of your own history. You step out from behind the fig leaves. And that's when love becomes possible again—not the fragile love of fair weather, but the deep, resilient love of covenant.

This is where the healing begins.

Chapter 6:
I Must Own My Side of the Street

She came into the room with a folded sheet of notebook paper. "I wrote out all the things I wish he'd do for me," she said. "But then I crossed out his name at the top and wrote mine instead."

He looked confused. She explained, "If I want a marriage like that, I need to become that kind of spouse. Whether or not he's doing it back."

It was one of the most powerful moments in their journey. She wasn't surrendering her voice—she was surrendering her control. She was choosing to lead by example, not by demand.

He later said it shook him. "She stopped fighting me, and I finally saw her. I didn't feel guilt-tripped. I felt invited."

We don't change our marriages by waiting. We change them by becoming.

This couple stopped trying to fix each other and started living out the marriage they hoped for—one sacrificial act at a time.

POWER CONVICTION #2:
Challenge yourself to live up to the marriage you desire to have.

That's right, this is your job. If your marriage is falling short of what you had hoped for, you must begin by making sure you are doing your part correctly. You can actually heal a marriage from one side...by first removing all the reasons your spouse is unwilling to do their part.

This is the second of the Four Power Convictions, and it must be embraced in its full and literal form. It cuts through excuses and delays and speaks directly to the core issue of personal responsibility. Most people who enter the process of marital healing begin with a long list of grievances and a deep desire for their spouse to change. But transformation doesn't begin with your partner's repentance—it begins with your own ownership.

There is a moment in every journey toward marital restoration when one partner realizes the futility of trying to fix the other. That moment, as disorienting as it may be, is sacred. It is the point when the real work begins. Because until I take responsibility for myself—my thoughts, my responses, my contributions, and my blind spots—no lasting change can happen. Owning my side of the street is not about blame. It's about maturity.

This conviction calls for a shift from reactivity to responsibility. Instead of keeping a running tally of your spouse's failures, you begin examining your own heart. You stop asking, "What's wrong with them?" and start asking, "What's going on in me?" It's not about ignoring your spouse's dysfunction—it's about refusing to let their dysfunction define your behavior. This one change will halt the tendency to get trapped into an *exit strategy* mindset, where all you think about is the delusion that life will be better *after* he /she's gone. Instead, you can begin to think about restoration of a true partnership once more.

The Trap of Blame

Blame is seductive. It feels powerful in the moment. It lets us believe we are righteous victims, unfairly treated and justified in our resentment. And sometimes, the pain is real. Sometimes, you have truly been wronged. But when blame becomes a lifestyle, it blinds us to our own agency. It keeps us stuck. It lures us into a cycle of self-perpetuating delusion of power, because, as an aggrieved party, we feel permitted to exact payment from the other person, while escaping any responsibility or culpability for our contribution to the actual dynamic or problem.

When you live in blame, you hand your emotional state over to someone else. You say, in effect, "I can't be okay until you change." That posture is emotionally disempowering. It makes your well-being dependent on another person's growth—which may never come.

Owning your side of the street doesn't excuse your spouse's actions. It reclaims your power to live with integrity, regardless of what they do.

It breaks the cycle of emotional outsourcing. It confronts the part of us that says, *"If only they would change, I could be at peace."* It calls us to recognize that peace doesn't begin with external changes—it begins with internal accountability.

Imagine a neighborhood dispute where each homeowner refuses to clean up their property until the neighbor does. The trash piles up, the fences fall into disrepair, and resentment grows. But what if one neighbor, without waiting for the other, simply started repairing what was theirs to fix?

The entire atmosphere would shift—not because the problem vanished, but because responsibility was restored.

In the same way, your side of the street is yours—not because you're at fault for everything, but because you're the only one who can clean up what you've contributed. That doesn't make you a doormat. It makes you a steward of your integrity.

This conviction is not for the faint of heart. It requires humility, reflection, and repentance. But it's also the door to real power—not power over your spouse, but power over yourself. The moment you stop waiting for them to make it right and start making your own part right, you reclaim your dignity, your direction, and your capacity to love with strength.

Boundaries, Not Barriers

It's easy to confuse responsibility with burden. You are not called to fix your marriage alone, nor are you meant to carry the emotional weight of two people. But you are called to take full ownership of your own behavior.

This is where healthy boundaries come in. Boundaries are not walls you use to shut people out. They are gates you use to manage what you will allow in and what you will give out. Boundaries clarify where your responsibility ends, and another person's begins.

My personal favorite explanation of a boundary is the line where I stop, and you start, and where you stop, and I start. A more contemporary saying is to stay in your own lane. When everyone respects that we have a space in which we are personally responsible, and a space where we are not, we are all safer.

> **A boundary is the line where I stop, and you start, and where you stop, and I start.**

When you own your side of the street, stay in your own lane, or in your own yard, you stop policing your spouse's emotions and start regulating your own. You stop trying to change their habits and start confronting your patterns. You stop using their shortcomings as justification for your reactions. You begin responding, not reacting.

That shift changes the tone of every conversation. It de-escalates conflict. It opens space for mutual accountability. And even if your spouse doesn't join you right away, the clarity of your self-ownership creates a kind of moral gravity that invites change.

Leading With Integrity

One of the most powerful results of this conviction is that it positions you to lead with integrity. Instead of waiting for your spouse to model maturity, you become the example. This doesn't mean you're morally superior—it means you're taking initiative.

Every healthy marriage needs someone to go first. Someone to set the tone. Someone to lower the volume, soften the edge, extend the olive branch. Owning your own part consistently creates an emotional environment where grace can begin to breathe again.

Consider what it would be like to take a road trip where just about everyone else on the road agreed to drive according to the actual rules of the road. You know, like they used to? We would all most likely comply and do likewise. Tempers would go down, stress would abate, and we could rely on others not to put us into unnecessary danger. Driving would become more pleasant.

But, if 20% of the people around you begin to weave, speed, and tail gate, become aggressive and road rage once more, what will you choose to do? Human nature tends to enter into a phenomenon of group think and self-protection. Like during the covid pandemic when people got into fights in Walmart over toilet paper. When resources look scare, or someone is taking advantage, we enter into a new mindset.

If those around you begin to go against the social norm, to behave badly, violate your rights, or take more than you are getting, you will likely match their behavior to compensate. You will seek to balance the scales. This reaction isn't random—it's rooted in how our brains are wired. Psychologists call it *social contagion* and *deindividuation*: when people see others acting selfishly or aggressively, especially under stress or scarcity, they instinctively mirror that behavior to protect themselves. Group norms shift, and even well-meaning people begin to justify actions they'd normally avoid. But in marriage, someone has to resist that pull. Someone has to be different—on purpose.

You won't get it perfect. You'll still lose your temper, withdraw at times, say something regrettable. But when you're committed to owning your side, you'll be the first to confess, the first to recalibrate, the first to seek peace instead of punishment.

That kind of leadership is contagious. Even if your spouse is resistant at first, the consistency of your integrity will challenge them to re-examine their own. Over time, it may be the very thing that opens the door to mutual healing.

Letting Go of the Outcome

Here's the hard truth: You can own your side of the street faithfully and still not see the results you hope for. Your spouse may not respond. The marriage may still struggle. But that doesn't mean your efforts are in vain.

Healing is not transactional. It's transformational. You don't clean up your part to force theirs—you do it because it's right. Because God calls you to truth, love, humility, and strength, regardless of how it's received.

The goal is not control. It's peace. Peace with yourself. Peace with your calling. Peace with the God who sees your heart and honors every step you take toward righteousness.

> **God calls you to truth, love, humility, and strength, regardless of how it's received.**

When you challenge yourself to live up to the marriage you desire, you become the kind of person who can love even in adversity. You become whole even in imperfection. You become free.

And that, in the end, is the beginning of true reconciliation.

Chapter 7
I Must Challenge What I Think I Know

He used to say, "I already know what she's going to say." And she'd reply, "You're always guessing my motives—and you're always wrong."

This pattern of assumption kept their communication frozen. He filtered every word through a lens of rejection. She filtered his silence through a lens of abandonment.

One day in session, I asked him to guess how she'd respond to something tender. Then I asked her to actually respond. His guess was a mile off. The room went quiet. It was the first time he realized how deeply his assumptions had distorted their connection.

From that point on, they agreed to stop reading minds. Instead of saying, "You don't care," she'd ask, "Help me understand what you meant." Instead of assuming she was attacking, he'd ask, "Was that criticism—or are you feeling unheard?"

They started treating each other like a mystery to explore instead of a case to prosecute.

And slowly, curiosity replaced contempt.

POWER CONVICTION #3:
Challenge your beliefs about your spouse.

If you are one to *mind-read* or declare what your spouse thinks or what they are motivated by, then you are also likely to be wrong more often than not. When you mind-read, you are normally completely wrong! What you believe you know about your spouse is based on your most recent assessment of them. It is inherently biased and cannot be trusted. It is based on feelings in the moment, not on truth, or even fact. Your beliefs will tend to assume the most negative or extreme possibility. This is due to an instinct that tests the worst-case scenario against the likelihood you can endure it. If you can face the worst, and can anticipate surviving, then any other possibility is less scary. So, you naturally look to the worst first. This is the fatal flaw in mindreading.

> *We don't just interpret our spouse—we invent them.*

Whether we know it or not, every spouse builds an internal past-present narrative about the other. We take fragments of behavior, combine them with current emotion, and draw sweeping conclusions. This is where assumptions become dangerous. We think we know what they meant, what they intended, what they're thinking—and from there, we react *not to the real person in front of us*, but to the story we've created *about them* in the moment.

This is the mind-reading trap: assigning motives without evidence, interpreting silence as rejection, seeing flaws as patterns, and viewing everything through a filter of our own disappointment or fear.

The problem is not just misjudgment. It's that our minds are wired to expect danger. From a psychological standpoint, we anticipate the worst in order to emotionally prepare for it. This is called *negative attribution bias*. If I assume the worst, I won't be caught off guard. If I believe they don't care, then I won't be disappointed when they fail me.

But this strategy, while self-protective, destroys intimacy. You can't build connection with someone you've already condemned in your head. You can't trust someone you've decided is untrustworthy based on your own narrative. Even worse, your belief about your spouse often becomes a script they feel forced to fulfill—because no matter what they do, you only see what confirms your expectation.

Trading Assumptions for Curiosity

What if, instead of assuming, you asked? What if, instead of judging the motive, you explored it? What if your first internal response wasn't, *"There they go again,"* but rather, *"I wonder what's happening beneath the surface?"*

Curiosity is a posture of grace. It holds back the rush to verdict and leans into conversation. It accepts that you don't know everything and acknowledges that your interpretation may be flawed. It treats your spouse not as a problem to be decoded, but as a person to be understood.

Curiosity sounds like:

> *"When you said that, what were you feeling?"*
>
> *"I'm not sure I understood—can you help me see where you're coming from?"*

"What did you hope I would hear when you brought that up?"

These are not interrogation questions. They are invitation questions—an invitation into your spouse's internal world.

Reclaiming Curiosity Before Rewriting the Narrative

Consider what you did when you first met your spouse. You were insatiably curious about them. You asked questions, listened with fascination, and studied every detail of their face, their laugh, their opinions, their dreams. You were intrigued by the way they thought, the way they told stories, the way they looked at the world. You noticed the little things. You delighted in discovery.

Think back to that first long walk or that endless conversation over coffee. You leaned in, not just physically but emotionally. You couldn't get enough of who they were. Everything was new. Even the quirks that now drive you crazy were once endearing mysteries. Why? Because you were operating from a posture of wonder—not familiarity, not assumption, and definitely not judgment.

In a healthy, vibrant marriage, you need to recapture that curiosity—and then keep it alive. Your spouse is not a static person. They are a living, growing, emotionally rich, spiritually complex creation of God. You will never truly know all there is to know about this special, complex, and incredible person you have chosen to partner with. And that is a gift. That's not something to resent—it's something to reawaken to.

Curiosity doesn't just reignite passion. It rebuilds trust. It says to your spouse, "I haven't stopped learning you." And more importantly, "I'm not going to reduce you to who I think you are when I'm hurt or frustrated."

Now—only from that place of restored curiosity—are we ready to begin rewriting the narrative.

To challenge your beliefs about your spouse, you must first become aware of them. What are the labels you've placed on them? What are the storylines you've built over time? Where are you mind-reading instead of seeking truth?

Then you must ask: *Is this based on facts or feelings? Have I confirmed this with them, or just assumed it's true?* Most importantly, *Would I want them to assume the same things about me?*

Scripture reminds us that love "believes all things, hopes all things" (1 Corinthians 13:7 ESV). That doesn't mean love is blind—it means love gives the benefit of the doubt. Love chooses to believe the best when possible, and only confronts the worst when necessary.

That shift—from suspicion to grace—can change the tone of an entire relationship.

What You Practice, You Strengthen

The mind is like a muscle—it strengthens whatever it rehearses. If you constantly practice suspicion, criticism, and negative forecasting about your spouse, that mindset becomes your default. The neural pathways for mistrust become deeper. You begin to notice every mistake and overlook every effort. You respond not to who your spouse is, but to the defensive version you've imagined.

But when you begin to practice curiosity, gratitude, and humility, your brain starts to rewire. You become more attentive to kindness. You notice effort where you once saw failure. You begin to experience your spouse in a new way—not because they've changed, but because you've taken off the lens of assumption and put on the lens of grace.

This isn't about ignoring real issues. Challenging your beliefs about your spouse doesn't mean dismissing harmful behavior or avoiding hard truths. It means refusing to exaggerate flaws or ascribe malicious intent without evidence. It means refusing to let your fear speak louder than your faith.

Love doesn't just believe the best—it invites the best. When you begin to believe your spouse is capable of empathy, growth, and goodness, you call those very qualities to the surface. Your faith in them becomes a mirror they long to live up to.

Moving Forward

Challenging your beliefs about your spouse is not a one-time shift. It's a posture. It's a daily decision to replace assumption with inquiry, judgment with grace, fear with faith. It is a quiet but powerful way of honoring your marriage—not by pretending things are perfect, but by refusing to be governed by worst-case narratives.

If you want your marriage to heal, start by changing the story you tell yourself about your spouse. Make space for God to reintroduce you to one another. And remember: the person you married is still there. They may be buried beneath years of wounds and weariness, but your belief in who they can become may be the very thing that helps them rise again.

Chapter 8
Defining My Marriage

He kept a mental ledger. Every forgotten birthday, every silent treatment, every time she didn't acknowledge his effort. She kept her own list too—his sarcastic tone, the nights he checked out, the time he said nothing when she cried.

Both believed the other was the problem. Both were deeply hurt. But neither could forgive, because neither one was willing to stop collecting injustices.

In one session, I asked, "What would happen if you stopped keeping score?"

He looked at her. She looked away. "Then who would protect me from getting hurt again?" she asked.

That question was real. It wasn't just about forgiveness—it was about self-preservation. But over time, they came to see that their lists weren't protecting them. They were imprisoning them.

They began to release the small things first—a snide comment here, a missed date night there. And as they did, something softened. The past stopped being a weapon. The present started being possible.

Forgiveness didn't mean forgetting. It meant refusing to make pain the foundation of the relationship.

POWER CONVICTION #4:
Start letting go of the things that your spouse has done or not done that has come to define you marriage, at least from your point of view.

Okay, this is the hardest one for sure...but it can and must be done! If you or your spouse has become an injustice collector, then your marriage will remain in a place of hurt, anger, and emotional thinking.

Letting Go of the Past to Create a Future

Every marriage has its bruises. Some are accidental. Others feel like deliberate wounds. But either way, those unresolved moments begin to accumulate—until they become more than memories. They become a lens. They color every interaction, cloud every attempt at connection, and over time, they reshape how we see the entire relationship.

That's how injustice collecting works. It's the quiet habit of tallying up offenses, of clinging to grievances, of revisiting old wounds with fresh pain. It feels justified. It even feels safe. But it slowly corrodes the emotional and spiritual foundation of your marriage. You can't build a future while clinging to a catalog of past hurts.

Forgiveness and the Cost of Bitterness

Forgiveness is not about letting someone off the hook. It's not about pretending the hurt didn't happen or excusing wrongdoing. It's about choosing not to let your mind, your thoughts, your time, or your soul become consumed with the hurts of the past. Forgiveness is an act of freedom—for you.

Bitterness is what happens when anger and pain go unprocessed. It doesn't stay on the surface—it embeds in the heart. Bitterness is depression nurtured and held on to. It calcifies your heart. It isolates you emotionally and spiritually. And it doesn't just change your mood—it changes your identity. A hardened heart is an ungrateful heart, unable to receive anything positive, loving, or healthy.

There's an old saying: *Holding a grudge is like drinking poison and hoping the other person will die.* But the poison doesn't affect the one who wronged you—it affects you. It seeps into your tone, your thoughts, your interactions. Over time, it can make you unapproachable. Unrecognizable. And eventually, you—not the person who hurt you—pay the cost of your anger.

That's why this conviction is so hard and so necessary. Letting go isn't about forgetting. It's about deciding that your life is worth more than what was done to you. It's about saying, "I choose healing over hostility. I choose peace over pain. I choose the future over the past."

The Illusion of Control

One reason people hold on to past wrongs is because it gives them a false sense of control. If I stay angry, I stay guarded. If I keep score, I stay safe. If I don't let it go, they can't hurt me again. But in truth, the longer you cling to the ledger, the more power the past has over your present.

This creates a marriage dynamic where everything is filtered through suspicion, and no amount of effort from your spouse can ever be good enough. Even their genuine attempts at change are met with skepticism—because the past still holds the microphone.

Eventually, this leads to a relationship where the only version of your spouse you see is the one who hurt you. Not the one who stayed. Not the one who tried. Not the one who is, like you, a work in progress.

To let go is to relinquish the illusion that your pain protects you. It doesn't. Grace does.

Forgiveness Is not Fair—But It is Freedom

Let's be clear: forgiveness is not fair. From a justice perspective, it doesn't make sense. Why should you release someone who hasn't fully apologized? Why should you lower your guard when they haven't proven themselves? Why should you make peace when they haven't earned it?

Because forgiveness isn't about equity. It's about freedom. It's about refusing to let your story be defined by pain. It's about taking back your authority to choose who you're becoming.

You're not forgiving because *they* deserve it. You're forgiving because *you* deserve to live with a whole heart. You're forgiving because God forgave you. You're forgiving because the person you're becoming on the other side of forgiveness is far more powerful than the person stuck in grievance.

Letting go is not a single moment—it's a practice. It will likely need to happen again and again. But every time you choose release over resentment, you carve a new path forward. You turn down the volume on the pain and turn up the voice of possibility.

The Trap of Injustice Collecting

When a spouse chooses to see only their partner's errors, they become blinded to their own. Over time, this sense of injustice can produce a condition called injustice collecting. In this state, the history of the marriage is subtly rewritten to emphasize the worst and erase the best. Acts of kindness and seasons of joy are dismissed or diminished, while hurts and failures are recalled in vivid, amplified detail.

This is where confirmation bias takes root—where we subconsciously look for and highlight the evidence that validates our pain. Eventually, a self-fulfilling prophecy begins to unfold. We expect negativity, so we interpret everything through that lens. We believe reconciliation is unlikely, so we stop seeing pathways forward. We decide separation is inevitable, not because it must be, but because despair has convinced us it's the only option.

Just like burnout, this state impairs judgment. The emotional weight becomes so heavy that even simple solutions seem invisible. Perspective collapses under the pressure of weariness, and feelings become disproportionate to the evidence. Everything feels worse than it is, and hope feels farther away than it actually is.

But the truth is: solutions often exist. They are not always easy, but they are almost always simpler than the emotional turmoil makes them seem. You must recognize that your heart may not be seeing clearly when it is overwhelmed with offense, fatigue, and fear. The decision to let go—to release the grip of injustice collecting—is often the first and most powerful step toward clarity.

Moving Forward

This conviction is not asking you to erase your past. It's asking you to stop bowing down to it. You will never forget what hurt you—but you can choose not to let it lead you. The goal is not amnesia. The goal is authority.

You get to choose which memories shape your marriage from this day forward.

> Will it be the ones that broke you—or the ones that healed you?

> Will it be the moments you were wronged—or the moments you reached out in faith?

The past doesn't have to define your future. But you do have to let it go to build what comes next. That's the power of Conviction Four. It opens your hands. It softens your heart. It clears the rubble so that something new can be built. And in that clearing, God begins to restore what once felt impossible.

This chapter may have asked the most of you. Releasing the past is not natural. It's not quick. And it's certainly not easy. But it is holy. It is the ground where real healing begins. You are not minimizing your wounds by letting go—you are maximizing your capacity for joy. You are reclaiming space for love, peace, and a future that isn't held hostage by yesterday's pain.

So take the next step—however small—toward forgiveness. Toward healing. Toward freedom. And remember: grace is not a reward for those who have earned it. It's a gift for those who need it. Receive it for yourself, and let it overflow to the one you married.

Let this be the beginning of a new story—not because the past is gone, but because you have chosen what will lead you forward.

A Bridge to Restoration: Introducing the Six Principles

Now that you've embraced the Four Power Convictions, you've laid a strong foundation for change. These convictions help clear the emotional and spiritual ground, uproot harmful mindsets, and realign your focus away from blame and toward responsibility. But conviction alone isn't the full journey—action must follow.

That's where the *Six Principles* come in. In the next phase of your journey, these principles will offer a framework for rebuilding connection, trust, and intimacy. They represent the daily, intentional actions that embody the heart of reconciliation. While each will be taught in depth in my companion volume, <u>Reconciled! Rediscovering Friendship in Marriage</u>, what follows here is a brief introduction to help orient your heart and prepare your next steps:

1. **Be Humble First** – Approach your spouse with a posture of humility, not entitlement. Humility defuses conflict and opens the door to healing.

2. **Offer Safety** – Emotional safety is the soil in which trust grows. Make your words and presence a refuge, not a threat.

3. **Listen for Hurt, Not Just Words** – Behind every harsh word or withdrawal is often a wound. Learn to listen with compassion, not just logic.

4. **Speak the Truth in Love** – Reconciliation requires honesty, but it must be wrapped in grace. Truth without love is brutality; love without truth is compromise.

5. **Take Ownership Generously** – Don't wait for perfect fairness. Take full ownership of your contributions to the problem—and to the solution.

6. **Walk in Consistency** – Rebuilding a broken marriage isn't about grand gestures; it's about small, faithful choices repeated over time.

These principles will guide the daily decisions that shape a reconciled relationship. They are not quick fixes, but heart-level commitments. And they begin now—one step at a time, in the strength God provides.

Now that the ground is cleared and the principles are before you, it's time to move forward. Let's take the next step together.

Chapter 9
Love That Does Not Wait

They came into session after a blow-up. She had taken the first step—again—and he hadn't responded the way she hoped.

"Why should I keep doing this if he won't meet me halfway?" she asked. Her tone was tired, not angry. Just worn.

He looked ashamed. "I don't know how to respond when you're kind. I always think it's a setup."

That was the breakthrough.

She had decided to love first. But she had attached a silent hope to it—one that expected a return.

When that didn't happen, it crushed her. He had received her love, but through the filter of past pain, he distrusted it.

*They both had to learn something deeper: that love, at its best, is a gift—**not a trade**. That when one person chooses to act in love, even when it isn't returned, it doesn't make them weak. It makes them courageous.*

Over time, he began to believe it was real. And she began to love without tallying results.

That's when restoration began.

A Future Worth Fighting For

You've done courageous work. By embracing the Four Power Convictions, you've challenged old patterns, confronted your own thinking, reclaimed your side of the street, and released the weight of the past. That alone is a miracle in motion. It takes honesty, humility, and a willingness to face hard truths. But healing is not only about what you walk away from—it's about what you're walking toward. You've cleared the weeds, removed the rubble, and now you are standing at the edge of what can be a brand new beginning. But beginnings must be built upon.

This chapter is about vision. It's about imagining, maybe for the first time in a long time, what reconciliation could actually look like for you and your spouse. Not perfection. Not pretending. But a real, vibrant, God-honoring relationship that's marked by grace, truth, and mutual growth. A relationship that's no longer dominated by fear, silence, or blame, but instead anchored in hope, intentionality, and love that chooses to stay. It's about a future worth the fight—not just for survival, but for joy, for legacy, for the sacred bond of two people choosing each other again and again.

When couples lose sight of the future, they stop building. They may maintain, or survive, but they no longer create. Vision is the fuel of restoration. It breathes purpose into daily choices and gives meaning to the hard work of change. Without a shared vision, the relationship is vulnerable to drifting. But with vision—even imperfect vision—there is direction. There is alignment. There is movement. It is vision that tells you why to get up and try again. It is vision that anchors you when emotions sway.

Marriages don't heal by accident. They are rebuilt by people who are willing to see the good again—even when it's buried beneath years of disappointment or silence. They are transformed by couples who, instead of rehearsing past offenses, choose to rehearse what's possible. Rehearse hope. Rehearse affection. Rehearse the kind of communication you want to have, even if it feels unfamiliar or awkward at first. Healing takes imagination—it requires that we dream again, even when disappointment has made us cynical.

Think back to the early days of your relationship. What were you hoping for? What made you choose this person out of all others? What kind of life were you dreaming of building together? Those desires may feel distant now—but they are not lost. Often, they are simply buried beneath pain. And just as pain has power, so does hope. It only needs a little light to begin to grow again. If you remember anything, remember this: you were drawn together for a reason, and while the journey has gotten harder, it's not over.

As you look forward, ask yourself: What kind of marriage do I want to create? What kind of spouse do I want to be? What kind of home do I want to build—not just for me, but for the legacy we leave behind? This is not about fantasy. It's about faith. Faith that God can do more than you ask or imagine. Faith that the marriage you long for isn't beyond reach, but begins with the next faithful step. Faith that your efforts, when surrendered to Christ, will not be wasted.

Reconciliation is not a destination—it's a journey. It requires new habits, new patterns, and new grace every day. It's not about pretending the past didn't happen; it's about choosing not to let it dominate the future. And it's not about waiting until everything feels right—it's about doing what's right even when it's hard. It's in those choices—unseen, daily, often quiet—that a marriage is restored from the inside out.

Your story isn't over. In fact, the most beautiful chapters may still be unwritten. The choices you make now—about humility, forgiveness, truth, and love—are shaping what those chapters will become. The pages ahead are blank, and that's not a cause for fear. It's an invitation. An opportunity to co-author something sacred with your spouse and your Savior.

You've come this far. Now take the next step. Not alone, but together. And not in your own strength, but in the power and presence of the One who makes all things new. His mercies are new every morning, and so too can your marriage be.

In our foundational materials, we offer a course called *The Chosen Marriage*. In that program, I encourage couples—and those preparing for marriage—to approach the relationship strategically. The idea is to *engineer* a great marriage, not settle into a typical one. After all, typical marriages in the modern era often end in divorce, heartache, drama, trauma, or all of the above. But it hasn't always been this way. As recently as your grandparents' generation, marriage was commonly seen as something stable, honorable, and enduring. It was meant to be special—not traumatic.

The problem is that too many essential pieces are missing from the so-called "typical marriage" today. To counter this, couples must begin thinking jointly about outcomes—what kind of marriage do we want to build?—and then construct a plan to get there. Most people simply live daily lives of happenstance, assuming marriage will naturally evolve into something meaningful. But that's not how it works, and it's one of the key reasons so many relationships fall apart. You must choose purpose over passivity.

When I was young, we often heard the phrase, "marriage is hard work." Our parents knew what that meant. But as generations changed and culture became more self-focused, the meaning got lost. Today, people think the hard work of marriage is about getting their individual needs met. But that's not what marriage needs. Marriage requires shared work, mutual sacrifice, and a shared vision. It requires a commitment to the "us" rather than the "me."

And vision is not a singular activity—not in marriage. It's a joint venture. It must be developed together, spoken out loud, revisited frequently, and supported with daily strategies and shared rules that keep it central to how you live. Without vision, even a promising relationship will wander. With it, even a struggling marriage can find its way home.

So don't just hope your marriage improves. Begin to engineer it with intention. Name your desired outcomes together. Create habits that support those outcomes. Revisit the vision often and revise it as life evolves. Set rituals, boundaries, check-ins, and celebrations that reinforce who you're becoming together. Make your marriage the most intentional relationship you have.

A good marriage doesn't happen to you—it's built by you. Together. And that building begins today—with faith, with courage, with clarity, and with grace.

PART THREE

Reconciliation and Renewal

Healing doesn't end with personal change—it extends outward. This final section explores how transformed hearts create space for friendship, peace, and the possibility of reconciliation. Whether or not the marriage is restored, you'll know you loved well—and that changes everything.

Chapter 10: What It Does Not Mean

When we first talked about loving without waiting, she got quiet. "That sounds like I'm supposed to just put up with anything," she said. "Like if he never changes, I just keep sacrificing."

It was a fair concern. And one I hear often.

Later that week, he raised a similar question. "So… I'm just supposed to be okay with her walking all over me?"

What they were both asking was simple: Is love the same as enabling? The answer, of course, is no.

Loving first doesn't mean accepting abuse. It doesn't mean hiding hurt. It doesn't mean tolerating sin. It means leading with the character of Christ—but it also means holding to the boundaries that protect what's holy.

This couple began to learn the difference. She stopped rescuing him from consequences—but she also stopped resenting him while doing it. He stopped justifying his detachment—but he also stopped demanding she pretend everything was fine.

They learned that love doesn't erase truth. It delivers it more clearly.

By now, you may be sensing the call toward a new kind of love—one that leads, rather than waits. One that offers grace even before it is earned. One that reflects the very heart of

God. But with that realization comes an important question: what *doesn't* this mean?

Let's be clear: this is not an invitation to lose yourself, suppress your voice, or accept harm. Embracing agape love is not the same as enabling dysfunction. Loving well does not mean tolerating abuse, enduring betrayal without consequence, or abandoning healthy emotional boundaries.

If your relationship has been marked by emotional or physical harm, this book is not asking you to ignore that reality. God is not glorified when His children are mistreated, manipulated, or made to carry the weight of someone else's irresponsibility. Love does not require you to set yourself on fire to keep someone else warm.

Love—real, biblical love—is not about being passive in the face of damage. It is not about minimizing your pain or pretending everything is okay. It does not call you to abandon discernment or dismiss the very real need for change and accountability in the marriage.

Agape love, the kind we are called to model, is *active*. It is discerning. It is holy. It always seeks what is best for the other person—and sometimes, that means saying "no." It means stepping back. It means creating space when chaos rules. It means refusing to be pulled into cycles of destruction under the banner of loyalty.

Sometimes, loving well means holding the mirror up—not to shame your spouse, but to call them back to who they are meant to be. Sometimes, love includes a boundary. And boundaries are not unloving—they are, in fact, one of the clearest expressions of love.

Sometimes the greatest confusion in Christian marriage arises when biblical love is interpreted as passive suffering. But even Jesus, full of grace and truth, often walked away from toxic dynamics. He confronted sin directly (John 8), set limits with the Pharisees, and refused to entrust Himself to those with manipulative motives (John 2:24).

> ***He never confuses mercy with permission.***

Loving like Christ does not mean letting people use you. It means standing firm in truth while remaining open to restoration. Agape love is not spineless—it is *spiritually anchored*.

Think of the father in the parable of the prodigal son. He loved his son deeply—but he let him leave. He did not chase. He did not prevent consequence. He waited with open arms—but he waited from a place of clarity, not codependence.

> ***That's what strong love looks like: firm, holy, and full of hope.***

Boundaries protect both people. They say, "I will not let us continue this pattern because I care about what we are becoming." They declare, "I will not enable you to remain stuck, and I will not allow myself to become bitter." They create room for repentance, for responsibility, and for genuine change to take place.

So, what does agape love *not* mean? It does not mean:

- Ignoring repeated betrayal
- Excusing emotional manipulation

- Covering up lies or infidelity
- Silencing your grief
- Pretending things are fine when they are not
- Making yourself the sole caretaker of the relationship's health

If you're wondering where the line is—between loving and enabling, between staying and self-erasure—ask yourself:

- Is my staying producing fruit, or just prolonging dysfunction?
- Am I offering grace, or absorbing damage?
- Have I confused peacekeeping with peacemaking?
- Would I counsel a friend to accept what I'm currently tolerating?

These aren't questions of fear. They're questions of **wisdom**. And God invites us not only to love well—but to love wisely.

Agape love is not codependency. It is not people-pleasing. It is not martyrdom. It is strength clothed in grace. And when you love with that strength, you may still choose to stay—but you stay with clarity, not confusion. You stay with purpose, not panic. You stay with both feet on the ground, rooted in truth, not swept away by fear.

You are not responsible for your spouse's behavior. But you are responsible for how you respond to it. Loving first doesn't mean enabling forever. Forgiveness doesn't mean forgetting wisdom. Grace doesn't mean you stop telling the truth.

And here's the most important thing: sometimes, the most loving thing you can do for your spouse is to stop participating in their dysfunction. To lovingly, firmly, and consistently say, "This is not okay—and because I love us, I won't pretend it is."

Laura's Line in the Sand

Laura sat motionless, staring down at the tissue in her lap. She wasn't crying anymore. She'd run out of tears.
"He says he's sorry," she whispered. "But nothing changes. He disappears for days, then walks in like nothing happened. And when I say I'm hurt, he tells me I'm being unforgiving."

Her husband had been caught in multiple emotional affairs over the years. Each time, he promised to do better. Each time, Laura extended grace. But each time, he manipulated that grace to avoid growth.

"I want to love him like Jesus does," she said. "But I'm starting to feel like I'm sinning against myself just to stay."

We sat in silence for a moment.

Finally, I asked her, "Who told you that loving him meant abandoning yourself?"

She looked up—confused, maybe a little angry.

"I don't know," she said. "I just thought… if I was truly Christlike, I wouldn't give up."

What Laura hadn't yet seen was that staying in harm's way isn't the same as staying in love.

And what she needed wasn't more endurance. She needed clarity. And permission to draw a line.

Agape love never asks you to become less of who you are. It calls you to become more—more discerning, more courageous, more grounded in truth, and more anchored in the dignity God has given you. That kind of love changes lives. That kind of love honors God.

One man I counseled was proud of his "unshakable commitment" to his wife. He absorbed verbal attacks, endured long-standing financial betrayal, and tolerated emotional detachment.

"I'm just trying to be Christ to her," he said.

But over time, his passivity became resentment. He wasn't staying because he was spiritually strong. He was staying because he was afraid to rock the boat.

> **He wasn't loving her as Christ would—he was enabling her to stay spiritually asleep.**

It took a long journey, but he eventually learned that the most loving thing he could do was confront the dysfunction as a leader in his household, to lead as Christ leads. Not with cruelty. Not with blame. But with truth.

And for the first time in years, she woke up.

Scripture calls us to *speak the truth in love* (Ephesians 4:15), to confront sin with clarity (Matthew 18), and to bear with one another—but also to *admonish one another* (Colossians 3:16).

> **Love and truth are not enemies.**

When we withhold truth to maintain peace, we do not preserve love—we prevent it.

> **Agape love is not afraid of confrontation. It just knows how to do it with compassion.**

As a counselor, I'm often asked by husbands and wives whether they should stay in their marriage. Sometimes they lay out what they believe is a compelling case for leaving—an affair, a breakdown in communication, emotional detachment. And yes, there are times when separation is necessary for safety, sobriety, or healing. But let's be honest: most of the time, the reason they want out isn't because reconciliation is impossible—it's because obedience is uncomfortable.

They say things like, "I think God told me it's time to leave." And I don't just nod along with that. In fact, I often look them in the eye and say plainly, "I don't believe you're hearing from God." Because the God who revealed Himself in Scripture is not vague about His position on covenant. He doesn't whisper contradictory impressions that override what He has already said in His Word. And He has said clearly: *He hates divorce* (Malachi 2:16). Not because He wants you to suffer, but because He takes covenant seriously—because He knows the damage that comes when we give up too soon.

God does not lead us out of marriage on the fumes of frustration or the fog of emotional exhaustion. He does not affirm our feelings by invalidating His own commands. His Spirit always aligns with His Word. If the voice you're following tells you to abandon a covenant without exhausting the path of repentance, accountability, forgiveness, and truth—you're not hearing God. You're hearing fear, or fatigue, or self-will dressed up in religious language.

Now to be clear, love does not mean enabling abuse. Agape love includes boundaries, confrontation, and consequences. Scripture tells us to *speak the truth in love* (Ephesians 4:15), to *admonish one another* (Colossians 3:16), to confront sin (Matthew 18). Love is not soft. It is strong enough to tell the truth and courageous enough to walk through it. If you're staying in a broken marriage, it must be because you're walking in obedience—not enabling dysfunction. And if you're considering leaving, you'd better be sure you're walking in the light of God's Word, not the haze of self-justification.

So no, agape love does not mean putting up with anything. It doesn't mean pretending. It doesn't mean lying to yourself to preserve an illusion of peace. But it also doesn't mean abandoning the vow you made when the feelings fade or the work gets hard. Consider safety as an action that takes the opportunity for your spouse *not to be enabled in sin against you* while he or she heals. Divorce is not necessary for this, but a timely separation might be. Separation may be long or short term, but it creates a safe space for healing to take place. Agape asks us to do what is *best* for the other person. Divorce doesn't answer that need. But space can. Remember, ask the right question, not the one you want permission for.

Agape love is costly. And so is covenant. But both are holy. And neither can be navigated rightly without submission to the God who authored them.

If you're looking for a way out, ask yourself—honestly—*Who gave me permission to walk away?* Because if it wasn't Scripture, it wasn't God. Leaving should be the most difficult decision you must make, not because you want to, but because you have no choice. The leaving is to help your spouse to change and heal, or to prevent your spouse from continuing in sin due to your presence. What it can't be is a way to get you off the hook. That is a difficult pill to swallow. But covenants should be taken seriously.

Chapter 11:
Your Heart Repositioned

When they first started applying the power convictions, they still argued. But something had changed. He no longer raised his voice. She no longer stormed out. They both started saying things like, "I want to respond differently," or "I'm trying to see this the way God might."

Six months into the work, I asked them what felt different.

He said, "I'm still frustrated sometimes. But I don't feel hopeless anymore."

She said, "I used to pray God would fix him. Now I ask Him to keep changing me."

That was it. The work hadn't magically healed everything—but it had realigned them. Their hearts were pointed in a new direction. Their love had become intentional, not conditional. And from that place, real growth could begin.

This is the power of a repositioned heart.

When you begin to live out the Four Power Convictions and embrace the posture of agape love—not as a feeling, but as a daily decision—you begin to notice a shift. That shift may not start in your spouse. It may not immediately transform your marriage. But it will begin in *you*.

This chapter is about that internal transformation—the quiet but profound repositioning of the heart that takes place when you align yourself with covenant love. Something changes inside when you stop waiting to be loved and instead choose to love from a deeper place of commitment, dignity, and spiritual clarity.

You no longer measure your actions based on what your spouse deserves. You measure them by who you are becoming. You don't operate out of fear or fairness—you operate out of faith. And in doing so, your heart becomes free. Free from bitterness. Free from the trap of scorekeeping. Free from the emotional rollercoaster of conditional affection.

When your heart repositions itself toward Christ and away from control, you discover that peace is not something your spouse can give or take from you. It becomes something that flows from within—rooted in the assurance that you are walking in obedience to God, regardless of the outcomes. That internal shift creates space for grace. It opens you up to patience, to mercy, and to kindness that is not reactive but intentional.

A repositioned heart is no longer obsessed with outcomes. It stops measuring success by whether your spouse responded, apologized, or changed. Instead, it sees success as becoming more aligned with the heart of Christ—who loved, forgave, and sacrificed long before anyone responded.

This transformation changes how you communicate. Instead of reacting defensively, you begin responding reflectively. You ask questions before making accusations. You listen longer. You seek to understand instead of seeking to win. You begin to cultivate a posture of curiosity over criticism.

This internal repositioning also softens your pride. You begin to recognize that your story is not just about how your spouse failed you, but about how you are learning to be faithful even in discomfort. You see opportunities to grow—not just grievances to air. You stop demanding, "Why aren't they changing?" and begin asking, "What can I offer that's life-giving today?"

You begin to heal.

And as you heal, something beautiful starts to emerge. Your presence becomes safer. Your tone becomes gentler. Your emotional life becomes more grounded. You become easier to connect with—not because your circumstances have changed, but because your posture has.

Even if your spouse doesn't respond, you are no longer controlled by that. You are no longer tossed about by their moods, their missteps, or their neglect. You're anchored. You've chosen to show up as the kind of spouse you were created to be—generous, grounded, guided by grace.

This kind of love is not weak. It's not soft. It's the strongest kind of love there is. It's the love that Jesus modeled. A love that led. A love that forgave. A love that stood firm. A love that gave all, even without guarantees.

And this is where you now stand—on the edge of something new. The old patterns don't have to win. The old wounds don't have to rule. The old fears don't have to drive. You are not at the mercy of the past. You are being invited to write a new story—not by fixing your spouse, but by repositioning your own heart.

This isn't the end of your healing—it's the threshold of rebuilding. The Four Power Convictions have laid the groundwork. Agape love has re-centered your heart. And now, as we look ahead, you are ready for the next chapter in your journey: learning how to build love again, one principle, one practice, one brave step at a time.

That is the work of reconciliation. And that is what we will walk through, together, in the book **_Reconciled! Rediscovering Friendship in Marriage._**

As we close this chapter, it's worth pausing to reflect on what proves real transformation—not just within you, but through you. Character, at its core, is the external evidence of your internal processes. People come to know who you are not by what you say, but by how they experience you over time. Habits. Reactions. Sacrifices. Your words may describe your *intentions*, but your behavior over time will declare your character.

Character is the external evidence of an internal process, demonstrated over time.

When you work on your own virtues—when you commit to raising your internal standards, and refining your thoughts, emotions, and behaviors—transformation begins. It may take time for others to see it, but the internal shift can be instantaneous. All that's missing is practice.

But for change to last—for it to become visible, credible, and dependable—it must meet three criteria:

1. **Appropriateness** – You respond to circumstances, whether challenges or opportunities, with wisdom, grace, and alignment with your values. In other words, your actions must become appropriate to the moment.

2. **Consistency** – You respond that way repeatedly, not as an exception, but as a habit.

3. **Timeliness** – You respond when it matters—when the moment calls for it—*and* that you stay the course over time to prove it is not a fluke.

These three qualities—right response, repeated response, and timely response—are what give weight to your transformation. They earn trust. They build witness. And they reinforce your identity as someone who is no longer reacting emotionally, but responding redemptively.

None of this is about your spouse's behavior. This is about your performance—your practice of becoming who God is shaping you to be. It starts with self-leadership. Self-control. Self-discipline. It's the hard work of shaping your heart to love with no excuses, no expectations, and no limitations.

> **Love is patient, love is kind. It does not envy, it does not boast, it is not proud. It does not dishonor others, it is not self-seeking, it is not easily angered, it keeps no record of wrongs. Love does not delight in evil but rejoices with the truth. It always protects, always trusts, always hopes, always perseveres. Love never fails.**
>
> *1 Corinthians 13: 4-8 (NIV)* "

That's what agape looks like—not as a theory, but as a practice. It's love in motion. Love lived out. Love that stands firm even when feelings fluctuate.

And in time, as this love is lived out through you, your heart—and your character—will begin to prove what your words never could.

Let me show you what this looks like in real life.

> *Cameron had been stuck in a cycle of blame. For years, he kept score in his marriage, tallying up everything his wife did wrong while excusing his own reactions. He came to counseling not to change, but to be proven right. But somewhere along the way—after working through the Four Power Convictions—something shifted. He stopped arguing to win. He started listening without interrupting. He began doing small acts of kindness without expecting anything back. At first, his wife didn't trust the change. But over time—weeks of consistent kindness, months of steady humility—something broke open in her too. Their marriage didn't heal overnight, but Cameron's heart had repositioned. His wife didn't believe his promises at first—but she couldn't ignore his patterns.*

That's how transformation works. Slowly, deeply, quietly—and then unmistakably.

Romans 12:2 reminds us, *"Do not conform to the pattern of this world, but be transformed by the renewing of your mind."* That transformation doesn't always come with fireworks, but it always begins with a **choice**. And Galatians 5:22–23 (NIV) reminds us that the evidence of God's Spirit in us is seen in love, joy, peace, patience, kindness, goodness, faithfulness, gentleness, and self-control. These are the *fruits* others taste when your heart has truly changed.

So before we close, pause and reflect.

Ask yourself:

> *Where have I been waiting for my spouse to change before I act?*
>
> *In what areas do I still withhold love based on fairness?*

What one change can I begin practicing today that reflects the person I want to become?

You are not just a spouse—you are a steward of your own transformation. Take that calling seriously. Let your heart be repositioned—and let that new heart shape your habits, your character, and your legacy.

Chapter 12:
I'll know I loved Well

When they first came to counseling, they were hanging on by a thread. Every week was a tug-of-war, every breakthrough fragile. But in the final session of our program, they sat a little closer. They smiled at each other. Not every wound was healed, but something was new.

I asked them both the same question: "What if your marriage doesn't become everything you hoped?"

He said, "Then I'll still be proud of how I showed up."

She said, "Then I'll know I loved him well."

That's the shift. That's the win. When your growth is no longer tied to your spouse's response… you've already won.

Because the point was never perfection. It was never even peace. The point was that you became more faithful, more loving, more aligned with God's heart.

And whether your spouse changes or not, you have.

Becoming the Change

As we draw this journey to a close, pause and look back. Not at your spouse, not even at your marriage—but at yourself. Reflect on the road you've traveled.

You've explored hard truths. You've questioned old assumptions. You've faced the tension between fairness and faith. You've wrestled with what it means to love first, to love without conditions, and to release offenses that have shaped your marriage for far too long. You've been invited to abandon the cultural scripts that treat marriage as a commodity and reclaim it as a covenant.

You have done holy work.

Whether or not your marriage has changed, *you* have. And that matters. Because you can't control what someone else chooses to do. But you can become the kind of person who loves well, forgives deeply, and leads relationally—even when the outcome is uncertain. That is power. That is maturity. That is Christlikeness.

What this process has done is reposition your heart. You've moved from blame to ownership, from resentment to responsibility, from fear to faith. You've embraced the Four Power Convictions not just as ideas, but as new standards for how you show up in love. You've begun to understand that agape is not about feelings or reciprocity—it's about embodying the kind of love that transforms lives.

But this is not the end.

In fact, this is only the beginning. Because now that your heart is realigned, the next season is about rebuilding love from that new posture. It's about establishing rhythms, patterns, and daily strategies to restore what's been lost—or to build what was never fully formed.

That's what <u>Reconciled! *Rediscovering Friendship in Marriage*</u> is focused on. But for now, the next phase of this journey will be more practical. You'll learn the six principles that form the structure of a healthy, restored marriage. You'll develop tools to communicate differently, respond wisely, and build trust deliberately. You'll stop trying to feel married and start *acting* married—on purpose, with clarity, and with love.

But for now, take this final moment to breathe in what God has begun in you. You are not the same person who began this book. You are stronger. You are softer. You are more grounded in grace and truth. You are ready—not just to hope for change, but to live it.

And remember: the greatest change you will ever make in your marriage is the one you make in your own heart.

The Unasked Question

A question I hear often is this: *"What if I do all this, Dr. Chuck, and my marriage still doesn't change?"* That's a fair question—but I'd suggest it may not be the *right* question.

When we ask questions, we need to first be sure we're asking the right ones. Because if we start with the wrong question, even a good answer can lead us astray. It can give us the wrong motivation or push us toward the wrong kind of action. So let's pause and ask: *What is the right question?*

What is the right question?

If your question is centered around, "Will this make me feel better?" or "Will this be worth it for me?"—then you're still asking from a self-centered framework. And love—agape love—calls you to something higher.

So here's the better question: *Will my change in behavior glorify and please God in my marriage and in my life?* And right alongside it: *Will my change in behavior be loving toward my spouse and honor my covenant?*

If the answer to both of those is yes, then you already have your outcome. Your obedience, your growth, your transformation—these are the things that matter most. And even if your spouse never responds, you are not the same. You've changed. You've chosen to reflect Christ. And that is always a win.

Now, if you still want an answer to that original question—"What if nothing changes in my marriage?"—I'd say what they say in the 12-step communities: *"If nothing changes, nothing changes."*

> **"If nothing changes, nothing changes."**

So what do you really have to lose? If your marriage remains hard, but you become softer, wiser, stronger—have you really lost? Or have you gained something eternal?

Here's the deeper truth: too often, the desire to leave a marriage is less about justice and more about fatigue or fear. It's rooted in a craving for ease—a hope that escaping the difficulty will bring relief. But relief without transformation is short-lived. A new life without new character will only repeat old patterns.

I hear people say, "God told me to leave." But if that voice is urging you to abandon covenant without first pursuing obedience, grace, truth, and transformation—then I lovingly question whether that voice is truly God's. Because the God who hates divorce (Malachi 2:16) is the same God who invites you into hard, holy perseverance. He may lead you through trials—but He does not lead you into self-deception.

So before you walk away from a marriage, walk deeper into your calling. Before you decide it's over, decide to become the person God created you to be—regardless of what your spouse does.

Because in the end, *your character* will speak louder than your circumstances.

Your change honors God. Your faithfulness echoes into eternity. And your heart—refined through fire—becomes the clearest reflection of who He's called you to be.

So, let's not end with "What if it doesn't work?" Instead, let's end with "Who am I becoming?" That's the question that truly matters.

> **You are becoming the change. And that changes everything.**

Six Months Later:

The Same Couple, A New Marriage

They arrived early again. But this time, they sat next to each other. There was no defensiveness in their bodies, no lashing tones in their voices. The room felt very different from that first meeting.

It had been six months since that first session. Their marriage still wasn't perfect—no marriage ever is. But the tension that used to fill the room was gone. They laughed now. They reached for each other without thinking.

"Things are… different," she said, smiling—not nervously like before, but genuinely. "I used to think we needed counseling to fix him. I had no idea how much I needed to grow. I mean, he hasn't suddenly become perfect. But I'm not reacting to every little thing anymore. I stopped trying to manage his attitude and just started managing mine."

He nodded. "Same here. I thought she was the problem. I thought if she changed, I'd be fine. But when I started changing, I realized—I wasn't fine. I was just hurt, angry, and selfish. I realized I was waiting for her to make the first move. To say she was sorry. To change first. But after walking through the Power Convictions, I had to admit—I was withholding love until she met my conditions. That's not love. That's control."

What changed wasn't just their communication. It was their orientation. They no longer looked at each other as adversaries.

They didn't see marriage as a contract to negotiate. They saw it as a covenant to honor.

She glanced at him, and this time, he looked back. It wasn't fireworks—it was familiarity. Warmth. Mutual effort. "I still get frustrated," she admitted, "but I pause now. I don't assume the worst. I ask myself what's going on inside me before I go after him. I'm learning to forgive quickly, not because he deserves it, but because I don't want bitterness to make a home in me."

He leaned forward. "I stopped keeping score. That was huge for me. I started thinking, 'What kind of husband do I want to be?'—not 'How can I get her to do her part?' Just doing my part, even when it's hard. Even when it feels unfair. Funny thing is… it doesn't feel unfair anymore."

She reached over and took his hand. "We're not done," she said, "but we're not at war anymore. We're finally on the same side."

And that's the beauty of this covenant-conviction focused work. It doesn't just repair marriages. It repositions hearts. It leads us back to the kind of love we were made for. Not love that waits, love that leads.

They looked at me, and for a moment, no one spoke. There wasn't a big breakthrough to celebrate. No dramatic story to tell. Just two people—still flawed, still learning—who had stopped fighting each other and started fighting for their own character.

And the results? They found peace. They found hope. And slowly, they were finding their way back to friendship.

Not because the marriage changed. Because they did.

"And now," I said, "you can begin to Reconcile!"

Appendix: Power Convictions Reflection Journal

This journal is designed to help you personally engage with each of the Four Power Convictions. These convictions are not just insights—they are invitations. They ask you to dig deep, reflect honestly, and shift your posture toward your marriage with clarity, courage, and compassion.

Use this journal privately or with a counselor, mentor, or support group. You may want to revisit it multiple times as you grow.

Power Conviction #1

Challenge your own beliefs about marriage in general, and about the current state of your marriage in particular.

Reflection Prompts:

- What are the unspoken expectations I have brought into my marriage?
- Where did these beliefs come from (family, culture, past relationships)?
- Which of these beliefs align with biblical truth—and which ones need to be challenged?

- How have my assumptions shaped my reactions?

Scripture to Consider:
Proverbs 14:12 — "There is a way that appears to be right, but in the end it leads to death."(NIV)
Romans 12:2 — "Be transformed by the renewing of your mind…"

Power Conviction #2

Challenge yourself to live up to the marriage you desire.

Reflection Prompts:

- What kind of marriage do I truly long for?
- What would it look like for me to live out that vision without waiting for my spouse to change?
- In what ways have I been passive, reactive, or conditional in my love?
- What is God asking of *me* right now, regardless of what my spouse does?

Scripture to Consider:
Ephesians 5:1-2 — "Be imitators of God… and walk in love, as Christ loved us…" (ESV)
Galatians 6:9 — "Let us not grow weary in doing good…" (ESV)

Power Conviction #3

Challenge your beliefs about your spouse.

Reflection Prompts:

- What assumptions do I frequently make about my spouse's motives?
- How often do I "mind-read" or jump to conclusions?
- What would it look like to get curious instead of accusatory?
- How can I create space for my spouse to be seen in a new light?

Scripture to Consider:
1 Corinthians 13:7 — "Love believes all things, hopes all things…" (ESV)
James 1:19 — "Everyone should be quick to listen, slow to speak, and slow to become angry."

Power Conviction #4

Let go of the things your spouse has done or not done that have come to define your marriage… at least from your point of view.

Reflection Prompts:

- What grievances or wounds have I been carrying for a long time?
- How have they shaped the way I view my spouse—and myself?

- What would it look like to release the weight of those offenses?

- How might forgiveness set *me* free?

Scripture to Consider:
Colossians 3:13 — "Forgive as the Lord forgave you."(NIV)
Hebrews 12:15 — "See to it that no bitter root grows up to cause trouble…" (NIV)

Appendix: False Belief Worksheet

Identifying and Replacing Distorted Thinking in Your Marriage

Our thoughts shape our reactions. And often, the pain we feel in marriage is amplified by *what we tell ourselves* about what's happening—not just what is actually happening.

This worksheet is designed to help you:

- Recognize distorted or harmful beliefs
- Examine their emotional and behavioral effects
- Replace them with truth—both logical and biblical

Step 1: Identify the Situation

Describe a recent conflict or moment of emotional intensity.

- What happened?
- When and where did it take place?
- Who was involved?

Step 2: Identify the Belief

Write down the thought or belief you had about your spouse, yourself, or your marriage during or after the situation.

Examples:

- "He never listens to me."
- "She doesn't care how I feel."
- "I always have to fix things because my spouse won't."
- "I'm not lovable."
- "Marriage isn't worth it."

Step 3: Examine the Emotion

What emotions did this belief produce?

Circle all that apply or write your own:
Anger | Sadness | Fear | Shame | Resentment | Hopelessness | Guilt | Other: _____

Step 4: Trace the Root

Where did this belief come from?

- A past experience (e.g., family of origin, betrayal, past argument)?
- A cultural or media message?
- A fear or insecurity you carry?
- A distorted theology?

Step 5: Challenge the Belief

Ask yourself: Is this belief absolutely true?

- What evidence supports this thought?
- What evidence contradicts it?
- Would I say this to a friend in a similar situation?

Step 6: Replace the Belief with Truth

What is a more accurate and grace-filled belief you can choose to act on?

Examples:

- "We've had hard moments, but he's trying to grow."
- "I feel unheard, but that doesn't mean she doesn't care."
- "I can choose to love today, regardless of what comes back."
- "God sees me, even when I feel invisible."

Step 7: Add Biblical Insight

Which scripture speaks to this new belief?

Suggestions:

- Romans 12:2 – "Be transformed by the renewing of your mind…"
- Proverbs 3:5-6 – "Lean not on your own understanding…" (NIV)
- Psalm 34:18 – "The Lord is close to the brokenhearted…" (NIV)

- Philippians 4:8 – "Whatever is true… think on these things." (ESV)

About the Author

Dr. Chuck Carrington, PhD, EdS, MA, is a Christian therapist, educator, author, and speaker with over 30 years of experience working with couples, families, and individuals—including trauma survivors, foster families and children, men recovering from pornography addiction, and the wives healing from betrayal trauma. He specializes in trauma, grief, and loss, with a focused practice in Christian counseling that emphasizes relational restoration in the wake of betrayal, infidelity, and emotional dysfunction.

Dr. Chuck's research explores innovative approaches to loss recovery, process addictions, betrayal trauma, post-traumatic embitterment, and the long-term impact of childhood family dysfunction. Blending biblical wisdom with evidence-based therapeutic models and a down-to-earth relational style, he brings compassion, clarity, and deep insight into how past wounds shape present relationships.

He is the founder of *Connect Christian Family Counseling*, where he walks alongside clients on their journey toward emotional and relational wholeness.

When he's not writing or counseling, Dr. Chuck enjoys reading, researching, leading workshops, and serving in local ministry projects. He also hosts free online support and discipleship groups. This book reflects his passion for bringing a practical, gospel-centered message to those navigating the complex challenges of modern life—helping them rediscover their identity and purpose in God's redemptive plan, and equipping them to grow in truth, strength, and grace.

If You Need Counseling or Help,

Dr Chuck offers Christian Faith-Based Counseling and Coaching in trauma, grief and loss, and specializes in men's recovery from porn and cyber-addiction, Betrayal Trauma recovery, and restorative counseling to help heal and recover marriages after betrayal, as well as workshops, online webinars and master classes.

For a consultation via telehealth video, contact Dr Chuck to get more information on how to overcome the damage of betrayal and addiction. Use the website below to sign up for recovery and support groups, or to join Dr Chuck's online psychoeducational programs.

If you are looking for marriage enhancement counseling or coaching, Dr Chuck offers online webinars and forums to help Christian couples explore their marriage, and how it conforms to God's plan for marriage, to find forgiveness and healing, or to plan for an extraordinary marriage from the outset for engaged couples.

Believers should ask for the Faith-based community discount for the best possible pricing. Free groups include Healing Hearts for women damaged by betrayal, Overcomer's Group for men struggling with porn addiction and cyber addiction.

www.connectcounselor.com
Connect Christian Family Counseling

Other Titles by Dr Chuck

Feelings Don't Care About Your Facts: How Emotional Reasoning Hijacks Logic

We've all been there—trapped in an argument where logic and reason are rendered useless, where emotions drive the conversation, and no amount of evidence seems to matter. This phenomenon is called emotional reasoning, and it can wreak havoc on relationships, leaving both partners feeling unheard, frustrated, and stuck in cycles of conflict.

In Feelings Don't Care About Your Facts, Dr. Chuck dives into the psychology behind emotional reasoning, exploring its deep roots in arrested development, betrayal trauma, attachment wounds, and narcissistic injuries. With clear insights and practical strategies, he unpacks how emotional reasoning takes hold, why some people seem so immune to logic in the heat of the moment, and—most importantly—how to break free from these destructive patterns.

If you often find yourself in arguments where facts are ignored and emotions prevail, this book will give you the tools to navigate these challenges, restore balance, and build healthier connections.

The Renewed Mind: Rebuilding Trust in Marriage by Overcoming Porn Addiction for Life

Unlock the path to renewed trust and lasting Christian pornography recovery with The Renewed Mind: Rebuilding Trust in Marriage by Overcoming Porn Addiction for Life. Whether you're embarking on a personal journey, seeking support in group sessions, opting for one-on-one counseling, or designing a church group for porn recovery, this book is an essential. Understand the foundation of recovering a man's self-esteem, functionality, and restoration of safety to his wife in a Christian marriage. Combine this manual with the companion Study Guide workbook and follow Dr. Chuck's proven 16-week process to complete recovery. With exercises and worksheets straight from Dr. Chuck's own counseling sessions, you'll conquer pornography addiction and rebuild trust, communication, and your marriage.

The Renewed Mind companion workbook

Bless Your Wife: small gestures to nurture your marriage.

Every man wants to be a good husband, strong, dependable, and loving. But too often, we overthink what that means and underestimate the power of simple, consistent acts of kindness.

In Bless Your Wife: Small Gestures to Nurture Your Marriage, Dr. Chuck to the hearts of Christian men who want to lead their marriages with strength, purpose, and Christlike love—but aren't always sure how to express it in everyday life. Drawing on decades of experience as a Christian counselor Dr. Chuck offers a fresh, actionable approach to strengthening your marriage one intentional moment at a time. This is not a book about grand romantic gestures or elaborate date nights. It's about showing up every day with a willing heart, an open mind, and a servant's spirit. It's about learning the language of love that your wife hears most clearly—whether that's a warm word of affirmation, a quiet act of service, or a moment of emotional presence when she needs you most. It's about doing the little things that mean everything. offers practical, easy-to-implement ideas designed to help you bless your wife intentionally and consistently so it becomes second nature. Whether your marriage is thriving, struggling, or somewhere in between, this book will meet you where you are. You'll find encouragement, insight, and a challenge—not to fix your wife or get more from your marriage, but to grow into the kind of man who reflects the love of Christ in the way he loves his bride. So, take the first step. Choose one small act of kindness. Then do it again. And again. Because when you bless your wife, you bless your marriage. And when you bless your marriage, you reflect the heart of God.

How Does That Make You Feel?: Why Modern Therapy's Comfort First Approach Fails to Bring True Change.

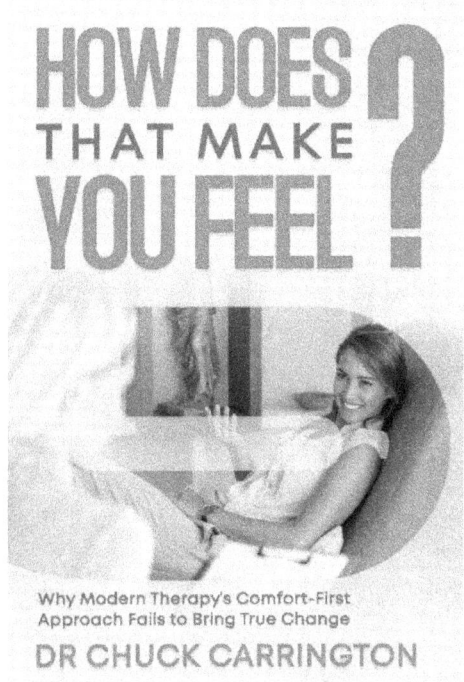

Are today's therapists helping—or hurting?

In a culture where feelings often override facts, modern counseling has lost its way. Instead of guiding people toward maturity and resilience, much of therapy now reinforces emotional over-dependence, encourages blame-shifting, and avoids the hard work of personal growth.

This bold and timely book pulls back the curtain on how the counseling profession—shaped by moral relativism, identity politics, **and** emotionally-driven education—has traded truth for comfort. It shows how therapeutic models stall out in emotional exploration, neglect insight, and sidestep action, leaving people stuck, fragile, and relationally broken.

The Forge: Where Men are Shaped for Purpose.

This is more than a devotional—it's a journey back to the anvil of God. It's for the man who knows something's missing. It's for the man who wants to lead but doesn't know how. It's for the man who's tired of pretending, tired of failing, tired of wondering if this is all there is. It's for the man who's ready to be reshaped. The Forge is designed to rebuild biblical masculinity from the inside out. Week by week, it will take you through themes of character, calling, courage, conviction, stewardship, and brotherhood. You won't just read—you'll reflect, wrestle, and grow. It's not about becoming the man the world expects. It's about becoming the man God had in mind when He formed you. If you stick with this journey, I believe God will meet you in it— not to scold you, but to shape you. Not to crush you, but to craft you. Because He's not done with you. Not even close.

The Masculine Edge: A Field Guide to Strength and Character

Discover the Edge You Were Born to Carry. The Masculine Edge is a bold, honest, and deeply practical anthology for men who want more than surface-level faith. Written with grit, grace, and gospel clarity, this collection of essays speaks to husbands, fathers, sons, and brothers who are ready to rise—not with bravado, but with purpose. Through field-tested wisdom, spiritual insight, and real-world guidance, this book challenges men to lead with strength, love with integrity, and live with unwavering identity in Christ. Whether you're building a marriage, raising children, or navigating brotherhood, The Masculine Edge is your field manual for intentional masculinity.

Dr Chuck Carrington
The Loving Marriage: Jesus Reduce Me To Love. Lessons on living out 1 Corinthians in Marriage. The loving marriage: Jesus reduced me to love.

In the second installment of marriage by design, "the loving marriage" the focus is on enhancing and guiding Christian marriages to their highest ideal. True love in a Christian marriage is defined by God, for God is love. Being truly loving to your spouse means being a godly spouse. Scripture provides a simple yet profound road map to guide all marriages on their journey of love, and in this book, we will  help you develop a personal expression of love within your marriage, rooted in timeless biblical teachings.

Marriage by design: the seven greatest hits in marriage counseling series by Dr Chuck reimagines marriage counseling by bringing his best practices directly to you in an accessible 21st century format. With live seminars, online groups, recorded video guidance, and downloadable materials, this comprehensive approach offers the most affordable and convenient way to strengthen your marriage without losing the personalized touch of live counseling. Doctor Chuck has distilled his extensive experience into the seven most impactful topics for healthy and successful marriages.

www.ingramcontent.com/pod-product-compliance
Lightning Source LLC
Chambersburg PA
CBHW032052150426
43194CB00006B/501